# HARVARD HISTORICAL STUDIES

## VOLUME LXXVII

*Published under the direction of*
*the Department of History*
*from the income of*
*The Henry Warren Torrey Fund*

Wellington Liberates Toulouse, April 27, 1814. A contemporary engraving reproduced with the permission of Musée Paul-Dupuy, Toulouse.

# THE WHITE TERROR AND
# THE POLITICAL REACTION
# AFTER WATERLOO

DANIEL P. RESNICK

1966

*Harvard University Press*

CAMBRIDGE, MASSACHUSETTS

*To my wife, Lauren*

# PREFACE

The movements of the Right that have opposed the legacy of the Revolution of 1789 to French political life are receiving increasing attention from European and American scholars. In France, where historical writing has long allowed the battles of the present to be fought with the materials of the past, eminent historians, like Professors Guillaume de Bertier de Sauvigny, René Rémond, and Jacques Godechot, have tried to rescue the subject of the Counter-Revolution from the arena of partisan politics. Their individual contributions have added greatly to our understanding of the dynamics of royalist movements and have stimulated wider interest in a study of the French Right. One effect of their work has been to call attention to the need for a better knowledge of the place of certain neglected movements in the making of modern France.

One of these movements is the subject of this study. The White Terror and the repressive measures that followed in the opening year of the Second Restoration first fitted out Bourbon monarchy in the trappings of reaction for a nineteenth-century audience. This early association of royalism with reaction was to do irreparable harm to the political future of the legitimist monarchical movement in France. Our study sets out to trace the sources of this reaction of 1815–16 in its southern bastions and to illuminate the process by which the new men in power sought to punish supporters of past regimes, redefine loyalty, and bolster the authority of an intolerant royalist faction.

vii

During the last century many writers had a vested interest in exaggerating the magnitude of this reaction. For certain men of the Right, this exaggeration provided confirmation of the thriving conspiracies with which the Restoration government had to contend, and justified *ex post facto* the repressive measures that were taken. For many on the Left, the excesses of 1815–16 somehow counterbalanced those of 1793–94 and the exaggeration of those of the Restoration left fewer to excuse from the era of the Revolution. Thus, it is not surprising that liberal historians like Achille de Vaulabelle wrote of 70,000 arrests in 1815–16 and encouraged the view formulated later by Odillon Barrot in his memoirs that "1815 can serve as a counterpart to 1793, and the White Terror did not differ greatly from the Red Terror." Ernest Daudet, whose monograph published in 1878 was the first and last on the White Terror, tried to dispel the myth of equivalence by downgrading the White Terror, which he described as a series of sensational incidents, limited in number and peculiar to the Midi. However, his emphasis on the spontaneity of the uprisings of the summer, and his failure to pursue a study of the Terror thereafter, in its legal and governmental phase, left questions about the origins and magnitude of the Terror unanswered. When Professor Guillaume de Bertier de Sauvigny published his first edition of *La Restauration* in 1955, he noted that it was still impossible to describe the White Terror with any exactness, since the necessary research had yet to be done. In a second revised edition, which appeared in 1964, he turned to my own preliminary findings for a description of the incidence of the Terror in its governmental phase.

I found research on the subject a difficult task. The absence of published statistics meant that the magnitude of the reaction had to be established from archival materials. Public and private deposits had to be explored with little advance promise of success and police and court records examined and compared. Parliamentary debates and legislation needed to be reviewed in the light of

## PREFACE

France's legal history and the complementary information that could be found in contemporary memoirs and correspondence. Secondary works offered little guidance in giving form to the material.

In this work, I received encouragement from many sources. First, I would like to thank Professor Guillaume de Bertier de Sauvigny, who opened his card catalog of Restoration materials to me, and offered advice on many occasions. Without the continuing encouragement and support of Professor H. Stuart Hughes and the additional counsel of Professor Crane Brinton, this work would have progressed much more slowly and would have emerged with many more flaws. Both read the manuscript in an earlier form, and suggested that it be revised for publication in the Harvard Historical Studies series. I would also like to thank Professor David Pinkney of the University of Missouri for his attentive reading of this manuscript in an earlier form, and to Professor Beatrice Hyslop of Hunter College express my gratitude for the helpful criticism that has made her assistance so welcome in this field.

The archivists and librarians of many private and public collections in France aided me in my work. From among this group to whom I owe a large debt, I would like to single out and thank especially Mme. Gille of the Archives Nationales, M. Robert Mesuret of the Musée de Toulouse, and M. Joffre of the Archives Départementales of the Gard. This seems an appropriate moment also to note my appreciation to Mrs. Alice Wemyss-Cunnack of Mas d'Asil (Ariège) for the text of the Ross reports, and her interest in the subject of this study. Finally, I would like to note how great a privilege it has been to have access to the holdings and services of the Widener Memorial Library at Harvard University.

Bronxville, New York                    Daniel P. Resnick
December 29, 1965

# CONTENTS

# THE WHITE TERROR AND
# THE POLITICAL REACTION
# AFTER WATERLOO

## THE FOLLOWING ABBREVIATIONS
## ARE USED IN THE FOOTNOTES

| | |
|---|---|
| A.N. | Archives Nationales |
| Arch. Pref. Police, Paris | Archives de la Préfecture de Police, Paris |
| Archives de la Guerre | Archives du Ministère de la Guerre |
| A.D.H.G. | Archives Départementales de la Haute-Garonne |
| A.D. Gard | Archives Départementales du Gard |
| Arch. Cons. Nîmes | Archives du Consistoire de Nîmes |
| A.D. Hérault | Archives Départementales de l'Hérault |
| F.O. | British Foreign Office |

# INTRODUCTION

All investigations of opinions and votes expressed before the Restoration are forbidden. The same disregard is demanded of both the courts and the citizenry.

—Article 11, Charter of 1814

The First Restoration was marked by a desire to bury the discord of the Revolution and Empire. This aspiration was evident in the terms of the new constitution, in the continuity of governing personnel, and in the absence of disruptive legislation. The great task of healing wounds seemed to have become the very mission of Louis XVIII and his entourage. However, to the genuine surprise of the moderate royalists grouped about the King, the regime was short-lived—its leaders forced to flee Paris at night as Napoleon regained the capital eleven months after his first abdication. What had seemed during the First Restoration like statesmanship in the effort at reconciliation was after the Hundred Days left open to the grave charge of treason. In fact, a sizable proportion of those in government and the military who had sworn allegiance to Louis XVIII the preceding year had rallied to the cause of the Emperor and accepted the Hundred Days.

Napoleon's efforts to regain control over the destiny of France forced to a test those who had so recently sworn to support the Bourbon government. Thereafter it became quite easy to distinguish the hard core of loyal royalists. Generally, only those

I

who had resigned from public office, taken up arms against Napoleon, or followed Louis XVIII to Ghent were considered among the faithful and trustworthy. The Hundred Days thus polarized opinion anew, suspending the growing rapprochement between opposing factions which had begun under the Empire. Moreover, it introduced a special bitterness by its arming of Frenchman against Frenchman.

In response to Napoleon's landing near Cannes, Louis XVIII delegated to his younger brother, the Count of Artois, and to his nephews, the Dukes of Berry and Angoulême, special military and administrative powers. The most extensive powers were given to Louis-Antoine, Duke of Angoulême, who was sent to raise an army in the South.

Angoulême's first hope had been to gain control of the Rhône valley, and this was the goal of army recruitment in its first phase, from the middle of March to the middle of April. The districts of Nîmes and Toulouse were the principal contributors of volunteers. At least 2,000 were contributed by the former, and the contingent from Toulouse may have reached the same number. Although these volunteers made up an important part of the royalist army, its heart was the tenth line regiment, the only unit in the regular army which remained loyal to the Bourbons.[1]

Welcome as the support of this regiment had been to the royalists, it made the formulation of a general policy toward the Napoleonic army stationed in the South impossible. Vitrolles, the royalist trouble shooter on the scene, described their problem this way:

The uncertain attitude of the troops remained our only danger; the regiments seemed to be just waiting for favorable circumstances to take a stand against us. This was the great difficulty in

---

[1] The tenth line regiment and the Royal Etranger contributed 5,000 men to the royalist cause, bringing the number of troops gathered in Provence in April 1815 to 10,000 men: See G. de Bertier, *Ferdinand de Bertier et l'énigme de la Congrégation* (Paris, 1948), p. 164.

our situation, to organize the war without the army and almost against the army, with the help of the people. Dissolution of the regiments was a thought that always came to mind but it was more difficult every day to take this extreme measure because the Duke of Angoulême had formed the nucleus of his forces from the army regiments.[2]

Around this nucleus the Duke of Angoulême had gathered almost 10,000 men. These troops were assembled by the beginning of April at a small commune near Avignon. However, they never saw open combat. In order to save his men from being overwhelmed by even larger forces, Angoulême arranged a truce with the commander of Napoleon's troops, General Gilly. The truce terms were generous and carried out before Napoleon could alter them. The royalist army was dissolved, without being effectively disarmed, and the men were given permission to return to their homes. The Duke was to embark from Cette for Spain, to remain in exile.[3] The Truce of La Palud on April 9 ended the life of the Central Government of the Midi and drove the royalists underground once more.

Gathered in northern Spain by the end of May 1815, several hundred French royalists under Angoulême's leadership awaited the circumstances that would allow them to return to France. In Figueras, a Catalonian fortified town, they were but 30 miles from Perpignan, and close enough to the Pyrenees to maintain regular communications with their partisans. They hoped to be joined at a decisive moment in Languedoc and Provence by other recruits to the royalist cause. These would be drawn from the ranks of the thousands then in hiding either to escape conscription under the Hundred Days or to avoid capture as deserters from Napoleon's armies.

[2] Eugène de Vitrolles, *Mémoires et relations politiques* (Paris, 1884), II, 393. All quotations from the French have been translated by the author.
[3] On the treaty of La Palud, see Henry Houssaye, *1815,* 10th ed., rev. (Paris, 1893) I, 422–429. Abundant references to the sources are given.

The five weeks during which Angoulême's provisional government exercised its civil and military authority in the South had established a familiarity with local grievances and a set of personal commitments that were useful to the Bourbon cause as southern royalists and their fellow conspirators in Spain began to plan the overthrow of Napoleon's government for the month of June 1815. While hoping to capitalize on any blow to Napoleon's power that might be delivered by the British fleet and Allied armies, these royalists planned to liberate southern France by their own efforts. Thus, plans for the reestablishment of royalist authority in southern France were made well before the defeat of Napoleon's forces at Waterloo.

# I

# THE INTERREGNUM AND THE
# LIBERATION OF PROVENCE

The public support that might be given to a royalist liberation movement in the Midi in June of 1815 varied from region to region. It was influenced by discontent with the imperial regime as well as by the positive ties of loyalty developed by the Duke of Angoulême and his supporters. Certain causes of disaffection among the populations of Languedoc and Provence under the late Empire had not been removed under the Hundred Days and these worked to the benefit of the Bourbons. The continuing economic decline of the two former provinces was still in evidence. The commercial difficulties of ports like Bordeaux and Marseilles, initiated by the Continental Blockade, had affected inland areas of small-scale manufacturing. Traditional import-export patterns had been further disrupted by army requisitions. In addition, army textile contracts in the last years of the Empire had been shifting to northern manufacturers, thus insulating large portions of southern France from some of the economic stimulus which the requirements of war might have brought.[1]

Other grievances were also by-products of Napoleon's war

---

[1] For recent surveys of economic conditions in Languedoc and Provence under the late Empire, see Jean Vidalenc, "La vie économique des départements méditerranéens pendant l'Empire," *Revue d'histoire moderne et contemporaine*, I (1954), 165–198; François Crouzet, "Le sous-développement économique du sud-ouest," *Annales du Midi*, LXXI (1959), 71–79.

needs. The conscription quotas, which occupied much of the administration's time, had been particularly heavy in the South. During the late Empire and the Hundred Days the *réfractaires* going into hiding to escape conscription represented a significant proportion of each levy.[2] Similarly, the rate of army desertions, which had begun to rise under the late Empire, had not diminished during the Hundred Days. In mid-June of 1815, just before Waterloo, the prefect of the Gard estimated at 1,000 the number of deserters in his department.[3] The mountainous terrain of portions of Languedoc and Provence provided a natural refuge for these fugitives, who moved about in bands that often terrorized residents of outlying areas.

The existence of these grievances on the part of the southern population made the royalist conspirators optimistic about the chances of overthrowing Napoleon's government in that region. As the Duke of Damas saw the situation later, their cause would have triumphed even without the defeat of the French forces at Waterloo.

His Royal Highness [Angoulême] received from His Majesty suitable instructions and full powers, and the effectiveness of the steps taken by Monseigneur [Angoulême] was such that, at the beginning of last July, even without the happy coincidence of the Battle of Waterloo, the King could soon have hoped to see most of the departments whose government had been confided to His Royal Highness again under his authority.[4]

The authority under which Angoulême operated from Spain had been confirmed by Louis XVIII's exiled court in Ghent on

---

[2] See examples of unmet quotas for December 1813 and January 1814, reported in the Bulletins de Police for those months and cited in Guillaume de Bertier de Sauvigny, *Un type d'ultra royaliste: le comte Ferdinand de Bertier (1782-1864) et l'énigme de la Congrégation* (Paris, 1948), pp. 102-103.

[3] A.N., F⁷9049, Prefect Roggieri to Minister, June 15, 1815.

[4] Baron [Etienne-Charles] de Damas-Crux, "Précis des opérations . . . ," MS in the Bibliothèque Thiers, Fonds Masson (Paris, n.d. [1815?]).

June 3, and the missions of Angoulême's delegates within France were inaugurated the following week. Their role was to be an important one for, in addition to organizing the overthrow of Napoleon's government in the South, they were to establish the cadres of a new provisional government in that region. As one of the delegates described his role:

My mission was to penetrate into France, as the special delegate of the King in the departments of the Gard and the Lozère, to bring royalist volunteers and the loyal subjects together, to make provisional nominations for all positions in replacing the authorities of Bonaparte, to overthrow the government of the usurper, and to gain recognition for His Majesty's authority by force of arms wherever there was no voluntary submission. Military operations were to be tied to a plan of campaign, insofar as circumstances allowed. But these operations were dependent on events and the local situation, since before acting, the means of acting had to be created.[5]

It may well have been possible for the royalist liberation of the South to have begun without the aid brought by Napoleon's defeat at Waterloo on June 18. Nevertheless, not until news of this defeat filtered back into France did the royalist movement in the South emerge in the open. The first important city to fall to the royalists was Marseilles, key to Provence. Thirteen days before Louis XVIII and his retinue reached Paris on their bumpy ride from Ghent the flag of the Bourbons was unfurled over the port of Marseilles.

Why did General Verdier, commandant of Napoleon's garrison in Marseilles, yield to royalist pressure and withdraw his troops from the city? An explanation for this decision is to be found in the local situation. Of some importance was the fact that armed

[5] René de Bernis, *Précis de ce qui s'est passé en 1815* (Nîmes, 1818), p. 9.

royalist gangs had entered the city. They had been organized the preceding March for the fight against Napoleon by the Marquis Charles-François de la Rivière, Angoulême's representative in Provence.[6] Despite the fact that these bands of royalist volunteers had been officially dissolved in April, they were clandestinely reconstituted during the remainder of the Hundred Days. During the night of June 24 they slipped into the city, ready to force the withdrawal of Verdier. At dawn they began sniping at troops from protected positions and even engaged in a light exchange of fire.[7] Nevertheless, there was no open battle to test the strength of royalist opposition. Thus, the violence of the gangs, though important, seems insufficient to explain the evacuation.

No doubt more decisive in forcing Verdier's withdrawal was the presence in the harbor of an English fleet under Lord Exmouth, chief of English naval operations in the Mediterranean. The English admiral had been blockading the port and it seemed likely that he would soon debark either there or in Toulon. General Verdier may have recalled the situation of Marseilles and Toulon in August of 1795 when the royalist cause in both these cities was advanced by the threat of Admiral Hood, then blockading the coast with English vessels, to enter one of the two ports.[8] Twenty years later the attitude of the local royalists to the English fleet was again friendly and communications had been established between royalist partisans and English vessels at sea.[9] On board his ships Exmouth had several English regiments along with contingents of Sicilian and Neapolitan mercenaries.

General Verdier's withdrawal left the city in the hands of a royalist committee which assumed provisional authority during

[6] G. de Bertier, *Le comte Ferdinand de Bertier*, pp. 168–170.

[7] Charles Durand, *Marseille, Nîmes et ses environs en 1815* (Paris, 1818), p. 7; Paul Gaffarel, "L'occupation étrangère à Marseille," *La Révolution Française*, LII (1907), 524–530.

[8] Jacques Godechot, *La Contre-Révolution, 1789–1804* (Paris, 1961), pp. 258–263, offers an account of this earlier episode.

[9] Laurent Lautard, *Esquisses historiques. Marseille depuis 1789 jusqu'en 1815* (Marseille, 1844), II, 340 ff., presents a legitimist's informed account of these events.

the difficult period that followed. The members of this committee, drawn from the local aristocracy as well as the business community, included few who had held public office during the Hundred Days. Nevertheless, Raymond, the one city councilor of the First Restoration to stay on in office during the Hundred Days, was allowed to continue as acting mayor. Caire, a lawyer instrumental in the formation of the royalist committee, was given the critical role of special police commissioner.[10] After the withdrawal of Verdier's troops, Caire became responsible for the maintenance of order. Under his authority were a newly constituted national guard of about 700 persons and a police force perhaps one-tenth that in size.[11] The events of the days that followed indicated that this force did not and perhaps could not prevent the excesses that accompanied the liberation.

The exact toll of the first two days of the royalist occupation of Marseilles is likely to remain in dispute, for inquests were not made after each assassination, nor were prison rolls accurately kept. On best estimate the number killed was probably about 50.[12] In addition about 200 more were wounded. These actions were taken in the absence of any official communications from Paris. A report received in early July, and left unanswered, brought to the Ministry of Police in Paris the first news of the occupation. A customs official, who fled the city on June 29 or 30, left a report in Valence with the prefect of the Drôme, who then forwarded it. This functionary of the Hundred Days in Marseilles estimated that on June 25 and 26, 250 persons had been killed or wounded, more than 200 put in prison, and 80 houses and stores pillaged.[13]

Lawless action in this period was directed not only at sup-

---

[10] For the composition of the royalist committee, see *ibid.*, pp. 347–348; Raoul Busquet, *Histoire de Marseille* (Paris, 1945), p. 382.

[11] L. Lautard, *Marseille depuis 1789*, II, 341, 346.

[12] On the nature of the casualties, cf. L. Lautard, *Marseille depuis 1789*, II, 354 ff. and P. Gaffarel, "Un épisode de la Terreur Blanche: les massacres de Marseille en juin, 1815." *La Révolution Française*, XLIX (1905), 317 ff.

[13] A.N., F⁷3786, Bulletin de Police, July 7, 1815.

porters of Napoleon but also at those whose misdeeds dated from the years of the Revolution. This is clearly illustrated by one list of those killed on the second day of fighting. Local chroniclers disagree on the completeness of this list but not about its representative character.[14] Of the victims, some had held public office, others were marked as informers or simply as profiteers. In addition, military men whose political sympathies were suspect or whose past deeds left unhappy local memories found themselves singled out for vengeance. Those affected also included two police officials who had been overzealous in tracking down young men trying to avoid conscription. Records have not yet been brought to light which would indicate whether these killings were carried out after sentence by an *ad hoc* judicial council set up by the royalists or as a result of direct action by individuals and gangs.

Among the slain of June 25 and 26 were many Mamelukes, regarded locally as Napoleon's mercenaries. The Mamelukes were part of an Egyptian colony of about 500 who owed their presence in Marseilles to the success of General Kléber in gaining recruits for the French cause during the Egyptian campaign. In the convention ending the campaign they were given the right to leave for France. Those who did not enter the imperial guard were garrisoned in Marseilles where they were joined by their dependents. Napoleon recognized them as crack troops, offered them good pay, and decorated them extravagantly. In Marseilles they had at first behaved as members of an occupying army and were not welcomed. Unable to accept their easy relationships with African mistresses and camp followers, the people of the city saw them as brawlers and profligates. However, the acquiescence of the respectable portion of the Egyptian community eventually permitted the arrest of the more flamboyant offenders in their number, and there began about 1807 a period of good relations between the Egyptians and the local community.

---

[14] Cf. P. Gaffarel, "Un épisode de la Terreur Blanche," pp. 317 ff.; L. Lautard, *Marseille depuis 1789,* II, 354 ff.

The period of good relations was not interrupted during the First Restoration and continued until Napoleon's return from Elba. It was then that relations quickly deteriorated for the Mamelukes were distinguished as active supporters of the Emperor during the Hundred Days. They should have left the city with General Verdier and the compromised local authorities who followed him. Their decision to remain, whatever its reasons, was a costly one. The Mamelukes were among the first victims of the reaction. As soon as the troops had left the Egyptians were chased into the upper section of the old city where many had made their homes. Those who could took refuge in the surrounding hills. After twenty-four hours the national guard intervened to protect them, but at least 12 had been killed that first day[15] and many more wounded.

The number obliged to flee because their names were on royalist proscription lists cannot be determined exactly. Nevertheless, as late as October, according to an unofficial estimate in police files,[16] 100 families still feared to return to their homes. Many officeholders of the Hundred Days were affected by these measures. A fear of retribution must have prompted their departure just as it influenced their decision to remain in exile. Those who did not flee were often forced to purchase their freedom in ransom or "insurance" from organized gangs.

While some individuals and gangs used unauthorized proscription lists as a front for their own efforts at extortion, the strength of the proscription drive, here as elsewhere in the Midi, lay in the movement to drive out "Bonapartists" from public office. The local royalist committee gave its support to the drive against former officeholders by approving the circulation of inflammatory pamphlets. The newly appointed special police commissioner, Caire, member of the royalist committee, endorsed the circulation of one such tract in mid-July. It demanded the pro-

---

[15] A.N., F⁷3786, Bulletin de Police, August 21, 1815.
[16] A.N., F⁷3786, Bulletin de Police, October 19, 1815.

scription of all officials who had not resigned their positions during the Hundred Days.[17]

In supporting this drive, the royalist committee sought to force a much more extensive purge of government personnel in Provence than the recently constituted Bourbon Ministry in Paris was willing to sanction. For example, a ministerial directive of July 20, signed by Secretary-General Barante for Baron Pasquier, had given the prefects great discretion in the replacement of local officials, but these changes were to be effected only where necessary "for public order" and were to be made final only with the consent of the Ministry.[18] The restrictiveness of this directive was attacked in another section of Provence by a lawyer at the Cour Royale in Aix.

It is impossible to emerge from a great disorder without great changes. The system of indulgence and moderation should stop. The agents of Bonaparte cannot be allowed to maintain their privileges and their jobs. Twenty-four million Frenchmen are opposed to it—and what circumstances can be more favorable than those in which the operations of the government are protected by a million foreign soldiers. There can be no error in the designation of those who are guilty. All Provence points them out.[19]

The first effort of the royalist leadership was to terrorize supporters of Bonaparte. To this end special commissioner Caire ordered the tracking down of all suspects.[20] It has been estimated that 200 were imprisoned on the first two days alone, and this number undoubtedly mounted in July. Usually brought to the jails by armed gangs taking justice into their own hands, the prisoners were held without examination or knowledge of the

[17] A.N., F⁷3786, Bulletin de Police, August 21, 1815.
[18] A.D.H.G., 4M36, Barante to prefects, July 20, 1815.
[19] Quoted in A.N., F⁷3786, Bulletin de Police, August 21, 1815.
[20] A.N., F⁷3786, Bulletin de Police, September 5, 1815.

charges against them. The prevailing political climate, the absence of examining magistrates, and the hostility of city mobs all seemed to indicate a gloomy future for them. Rumors were current that the prisons were going to be invaded and the "guilty ones" dealt with privately. City mobs threatened to open prisons and take their own vengeance on the suspects.[21] The prefect appointed on July 10 by Angoulême's special delegate, La Rivière, remained in office for a full month without making an effort to improve the lot of political prisoners. Belatedly, a prefect appointed by the new Ministry in Paris took office in mid-August.[22]

By early September, with a moderate prefect in office, the situation of political prisoners improved somewhat. One of the new prefect's decisions was to hold a public review of all prisoners held in the central prison of Marseilles. In two six-hour sessions begun on September 2, all the detained persons were examined. The dramatic intervention of the prefect in this judicial proceeding was testimony to the continued absence of judges from their posts and to their intimidation by the more outspoken elements in the royalist camp. Nevertheless, the prefect's description of this proceeding suggests that in his view the climate of political life in Marseilles had become calmer:

I had those whom it was decided would be released remain in the room, and I freed them myself, in the presence of the common people, who showed their satisfaction with this act of justice by their cries of "Vive le Roi!" [23]

We should, however, be cautious in our inferences from testimony of this kind. The prefect entered only the central prison

[21] A.N., F⁷3786, Bulletin de Police, September 13, 1815, citing prefectoral report of September 7, 1815.

[22] See A.N., F¹ᵃ95⁴. Vaublanc, former prefect of the Moselle, and later to become Minister of the Interior, was named prefect of the Bouches-du-Rhône on July 12, 1815.

[23] A.N., F⁷3786, Bulletin de Police, September 5, 1815, quoting prefectoral report of August 29, 1815.

in Marseilles. The outlying military fortresses like the Chateau d'If were not on his list and we do not know how many prisoners were detained there. Moreover, a trip to Tarascon for a review of prisoners was postponed because it was hard to find a magistrate willing to conduct the examinations. Some 60 political prisoners were reported held there, but neither their fate. nor that of those still detained in Marseilles, was revealed.

During the following month, when the political reaction was being controlled and directed from Paris and was proceeding according to legal forms, Marseilles was still terrorized by royalist gangs who were pillaging homes and shops. The lieutenant-general of police wrote from Marseilles on October 12, that the individuals involved were the same as those responsible for the first excesses in June. "The rallying cry is to massacre the Bonapartists and pillage their homes." [24] The disorders of June 25 and 26 were not, however, repeated on the same scale. By October the dominant voices on the royalist committee were those of local business interests. These men were clearly interested in preserving property, as a declaration from them on June 27 had indicated.

It is time that order return, and that men who are not natives of our city or who are trouble-makers, cease to profit from the tumult to commit crimes. It is time that person and property be respected.[25]

Nevertheless, the city's royalists had allied themselves with criminals and deserters who, once introduced within the walls, were not easily disarmed.

The success of the royalists in Marseilles brought to France the absent members of Angoulême's new provisional government for

[24] A.N., F⁷3786, Bulletin de Police, October 19, 1815.
[25] L. Lautard, *Marseille depuis 1789,* II, 364, cites the text of this proclamation.

the Midi. Although that government was not officially proclaimed until July 20, plans for its composition had been made
in Spain during the Hundred Days. Below the level of the chief
administrators were the special delegates, each of whom had one
or more departments under his jurisdiction. In addition to the
Marquis de la Rivière for the Bouches-du-Rhône, these included
the Count René de Bernis for the Gard, Marshal Dominique de
Pérignon for the Haute-Garonne, and the Marquis de Montcalm
for the Hérault.[26]

The royalist committee of Marseilles helped to further the
plans of Angoulême and his delegates by extending the liberation movement to adjacent areas of Provence and Languedoc. No
sooner had the city of Marseilles passed into royalist hands than
it became the spiritual and military patron of other royalist uprisings. The royalist committee attempted to rouse public opinion
in nearby departments by a proclamation that was a veritable call
to arms. In the name of the King, the committee called on
Frenchmen to be loyal to the royalist cause: "Provence and all
the Midi will become, if necessary, a new Vendée, rather than
fall back under the yoke of despotism or factions."[27]

The military arrangements made after the liberation of Marseilles laid the basis for a march on the port city of Toulon, some
40 miles away, and for the extension of royalist authority into
the Var. The royalist committee in Marseilles feared that Brune's
army in Toulon would march directly on Marseilles, or isolate
it by taking Aix. To forestall these moves they made the capture
of Toulon their next objective. Three men were to lead the march
and their authority was confirmed by La Rivière on his arrival.
The royalist leaders established as military posts four villages on

---

[26] Pérignon's role is discussed in Chapter 2, and that of Bernis in Chapter 3.
The activities of the Marquis de Montcalm in the Hérault have not been docu-
mented here.

[27] See A.N., F⁷9049, mayor of Nîmes to Minister, June 27, 1815, for a copy of
the proclamation. The same text is cited in L. Lautard, *Marseille depuis 1789*,
II, 350.

the route to Toulon—le Beausset, le Castelet, Bandol, and la Cadière. Royalists from Marseilles were not able, however, with the means at their disposal, to force a capitulation from the obdurate Marshal Brune, who commanded a garrison of at least three thousand men in Toulon. Even when 5,000 troops under English command began their debarkation at Marseilles on July 11, Brune showed no signs of yielding.

Brune did not at first accept the reports of defeat at Waterloo as accurate. Later, when news of Napoleon's abdication arrived, he showed his continuing loyalty by proclaiming the Emperor's son as successor. Not until news reached him about the Allies' dissolution of Napoleon's Army of the Loire did he finally capitulate. On July 24, 16 days after Louis' arrival in Paris and almost a month after the royalist occupation of Marseilles, he agreed to withdraw his troops.[28] In the meantime the royalist negotiators had been patient. General Hudson-Lowe, later to be Napoleon's captor, was not called upon to open the gates of Toulon with English cannon.

The Terror in Toulon began after Brune's evacuation and continued through the month of August. The pattern was not different from that in other cities of Provence. Royalist bands, largely from Marseilles, had a virtual monopoly of authority and force in the city. The absence of some public officials and the weakness of others had given the incoming bands a free hand. Prefect and magistrates had withdrawn; the subprefect in Toulon had allowed himself to be intimidated and the moderate mayor of a nearby commune had been forced out of office.[29] Justice was meted out within the city by a royalist military commission. Arrests and proscriptions were widespread and apparently uncontested. Austrian troops occupying the northern section of the Var

---

[28] See Ernest Daudet, *La Terreur Blanche: Episodes et souvenirs de la réaction dans le midi en 1815,* 2nd ed. (Paris, 1906), pp. 166–175, for an appreciation of Brune's position as revealed through correspondence at the Archives de Guerre.

[29] A.N., F⁷3786, Bulletins de Police of September 10 and September 12, 1815.

kept a hands-off policy on Toulon, hoping perhaps that a further breakdown of public order would give them the pretext they sought to occupy the port.[30]

The Terror in Toulon, like that which took place in Marseilles, was marked by a suspension of due process and a wave of arbitrary arrests. A military commission continued to mete out justice in the five weeks after Brune's evacuation of the city. One contemporary estimate set the figure of those in jail or sought for arrest at 800 men and 55 women.[31] Among those sought were purchasers of nationalized property during the Revolution as well as men who had remained in office during the Hundred Days. All who had joined the Bonapartist *fédérations* during the Hundred Days were considered suspect. Many decided to flee the city, and the number who had left by the end of August reached 1,000.[32]

The resumption of office by those appointees of the First Restoration who had resigned during the Hundred Days did not contribute appreciably to restoring respect for public authority. The harassed lieutenant of police in Toulon felt that several of these men actually contributed to the disorder.[33] What seems clear is that, in attempting to maintain their authority, these returning officials avoided making unpopular decisions. Reports conveyed to civilian authorities in Paris indicated that the result of this inaction was to place effective authority in Toulon in the hands of local royalists whose leadership and methods were hidden from the public.

---

[30] Report from lieutenant extraordinaire de police to Minister, August 22, 1815, summarized in A.N., F⁷3786, Bulletin de Police, August 30, 1815. For a discussion of the occupation protocols, see Robert André, *L'occupation de la France par les alliés en 1815 (juillet-novembre)* (Paris, 1924), pp. 51 ff. Félix Ponteil, *La chute de Napoléon et la crise française de 1814-15* (Paris, 1943), contains a schematic map of the occupation zones.

[31] A.N., F⁷3786, Bulletins de Police of August 27 and August 30, 1815.

[32] Charles Alleaume, "La Terreur Blanche dans le Var," *Bulletin de la Société d'études scientifiques et archéologiques de Draguignan*, XLV (1944-45), 7.

[33] *Ibid.*, p. 10.

Royal ordinance, ministerial instructions, nothing is of any value: everything is run by secret instructions. That, at least, is the general impression.[34]

The surrender of Toulon was followed shortly by the murder of its defender, Marshal Brune. He was the first of two Marshals of the Empire to perish in the reaction of 1815–16. Against the advice of his aides, Brune had decided to pass through Avignon on his way to Paris, and had been provided with a safe-conduct by La Rivière. Avignon was known to be in royalist hands at the time and to have, like Marseilles, an urban population violently hostile to the Empire.

In Avignon royalist mobs made their own law. "More than 130 persons, supposed *fédérés,* have been brought into the prisons of Avignon," wrote the acting prefect, who did not know if he could protect them against a hostile mob.[35] The mob had showed its power in an incident a few days before Brune's arrival. A man being taken to jail as a Bonapartist suspect had been killed en route by an assassin's bullet. The murderer was caught and put in jail, but the day following his imprisonment he was freed by a protesting crowd of 300.

It was impossible to put down the crowd, wrote the prefect, when the only armed unit that could be called upon, that of 200 national guards, had been sent outside the city on a special mission. Brune entered Avignon the day after the prefect had acknowledged his powerlessness: "When we have a force strong enough to oppose this agitation and exasperation of the common people, justice will resume its course." [36]

Had it not been for the literal adherence to protocol of a guard at his check-post, Brune might have been allowed to proceed up

[34] A.N., F⁷3786, Bulletin de Police, August 30, 1815.
[35] Quoted in A.N., F⁷3786, Bulletin de Police, August 3, 1815.
[36] Quoted in A.N., F⁷3786, Bulletin de Police, August 8, 1815.

the Rhône valley without detouring through the heart of Avignon. As it was, he was made to pull up his carriage in the square opposite the Hôtel de Ville. There his papers were examined by the local authorities. Cries of "Death to Brune" were heard as the Marshal was recognized in the streets. Despite the intervention of the mayor and the prefect he was waylaid as he tried to leave the city. The attack was savage but he was allowed to withdraw to a hotel. Shortly afterwards he was attacked again in his hotel, and dragged to the streets. His body was tossed into the Rhône, where it was to wash up twice before receiving final burial.[37]

[37] See A.N., F⁷9248, for two bound registers. These include depositions taken after the event, medical reports, and the letters found in his hotel room. One person was condemned, *in absentio,* in proceedings instituted by Brune's wife in 1819.

# II

# ULTRA-ROYALIST POLITICS
# IN TOULOUSE

I doubt very much that Paris, in the days that followed February 24, 1848, was more deprived of guarantees of order than Toulouse from the end of June to the beginning of September 1815.
—Ch. de Rémusat, *Mémoires de ma vie*, I, 220

The authority of the rural aristocracy in the Southwest, so important for the royalist cause in the summer of 1815, had been favored from 1807 on by specific policies of Napoleon. At that time the Emperor brought certain rural notables out of the exile of their estates into political positions at the village and department level. Such a policy in local government was, of course, but one aspect of a continuing rapprochement with the aristocracy of the Old Regime.

Joseph de Villèle, who later headed a Ministry for five consecutive years during the Second Restoration, was one of the principal beneficiaries of this policy. His political career began in 1807, when the prefect of the department appointed him mayor of Morvilles, a commune in which his family had been resident proprietors since the late fourteenth century. As Villèle noted in his memoirs, such appointments were a matter of policy:

All the land-owning notables of the department were also members of this [departmental] council, and at the Restoration, seven years later, we were still there. There had evidently been some general instructions to the prefects to give preference in their choices to the most important of the older proprietors in each locality. Bonaparte was aware that most of them were what was later to be called legitimists, but he himself said, "Such people cannot wish to see the earth shake." [1]

Landowners like Villèle, in the Haute-Garonne, found that people in the countryside about them had little loyalty to Bonaparte. Throughout the Peninsular War (1808–1814) and especially during the campaigns against Russia and the Fourth Coalition (1812–1814), requisitions as well as heavy conscription quotas had widened the gulf between the central government and the people of the Southwest. The interruption of the normal traffic of grain and cattle into Spain, necessitated by the requirements of war, alienated both growers and middlemen. In addition, to meet the requirements of the army, grain and hay had to be shipped long distances. These transactions required the services of a *fournisseur,* who seldom gave the farmers full value for their crops.[2]

The city of Toulouse, the most important commercial center in the region and capital of the Haute-Garonne, had been severely affected by these measures, since much of the profit of its commerce was derived from transactions in livestock and grain. The interference with that trade by requisitions may have had effects as grave as those imposed by the severance of commercial ties with England in the Continental Blockade. Toulouse was, at that time, still a city of shops and small workshops. Unlike the cities of Agen and Montauban it had no large class of workers

---

[1] Joseph de Villèle, *Mémoires et Correspondance* (Paris, 1888), I, 189–190.

[2] Complaints against this policy were registered during the Hundred Days: See J. de Villèle, *Mémoires,* I, 190–191. For the extent of the restrictions, see A.D.H.G., 4M34, district director of customs to prefect, May 4, 1815; Minister of Interior Carnot to prefect, May 9, 1815.

economically dependent on the activity of a single industry.[3] The short-lived textile activities of Boyer-Fonfrède were exceptional for their magnitude.[4] The Southwest began to suffer an economic lag in this period from which it did not recover for over a century.[5]

Royalist conspirators under the Empire were not daring enough or well enough organized to liberate Toulouse by themselves[6] but they gave their English liberator convincing evidence of royalist sentiment in the district. When the Duke of Wellington entered Toulouse on April 27, 1814, he received a hero's welcome.[7] His arrival allowed the royalist groups, organized earlier and in secrecy, to agitate openly for the return of the Bourbons. Wellington, however, maintained the same façade of political neutrality he had shown in Bordeaux the preceding month. As long as the British Government and her allies were negotiating with Napoleon at Châtillon-sur-Seine, he refused to give open support to a political faction. He did, nevertheless, permit demonstrations. The population, wearied and disillusioned by wars, commercial difficulties, and conscription, turned out in large numbers to give their support for a restoration of the Bour-

---

[3] As late as 1825, 192 different enterprises of thirty-six different types employed in all only 951 workers, an average of less than five per workshop. See Philippe Wolff, *Histoire de Toulouse* (Toulouse, 1958), pp. 348–349.

[4] See Henri Causse, "Un industriel Toulousain au temps de la Révolution et de l'Empire: François-Bernard Boyer-Fonfrède (1767–?)," *Annales du Midi,* LXIX (1957), 121–133.

[5] See François Crouzet, "Sous-développement économique du sud-ouest," *Annales du Midi,* LXXI (1959), 71–79.

[6] This weakness was manifest in the planning to capture Rodez in March 1814. See G. de Bertier de Sauvigny, *Un type d'ultra-royaliste: le comte Ferdinand de Bertier et l'énigme de la Congrégation* (Paris, 1948), pp. 111–118.

[7] A contemporary etching, used as the frontispiece in this book, shows the Duke on a white horse receiving flowers and cheers from the crowd. There is no doubt that a substantial portion of the city's population welcomed the end of the Empire. They would greet the liberation at the end of the Hundred Days with the same enthusiasm.

bons. In Toulouse, as in Bordeaux earlier, the British general was greeted with cries of "Vive Louis XVIII! Vive Wellington!" [8]

The Duke of Angoulême's provisional government in the Midi, established at the departing King's request during the Hundred Days, was based in Toulouse.[9] Angoulême's officials relied heavily on the prefects who had sworn their loyalty to Louis XVIII and the Charter. In cooperation with the departmental councils of the strongly royalist southern departments prefects took the necessary measures to support royal authority. Where possible, in the departments under Angoulême's jurisdiction, mail communications and money transfers to Paris were interrupted and Toulouse supplanted Paris as the source of civil and military authority for the region.[10] The royal authority in Toulouse characterized itself as the *Gouvernement Central du Midi*[11] and assumed a monopoly of legitimate authority in the South until Angoulême's capitulation at La Palud.

During the subsequent period of Angoulême's exile in Spain, royalist committees planned for the day when a secret battalion could be called on to take over Toulouse and aid in the liberation of the Southwest. In Toulouse itself the creation of such a corps had to take place under the eyes of General Decaen, commander of the tenth military division; his troops controlled the city. With the connivance of police inspectors, however, two companies were created by May 15. In these secret companies, called *gardes royaux secrets,* or simply *secrets,* were many men drawn from the periphery of society. As the Count de Chazelles described the re-

[8] See Wellington, *Supplementary Despatches* (London, 1863), XI, 630–631, cited also in G. de Bertier, *Le comte Ferdinand de Bertier,* p. 141. G. de Bertier, in the same work, pp. 126–142, provides a description of the planning and background of royalist demonstrations in Bordeaux and Toulouse, organized by the Chevaliers de la Foi.

[9] Eugène François de Vitrolles, *Mémoires et relations politiques* (Paris, 1884), II, 383–401, gives a description of some of its functions.

[10] Correspondence between Vitrolles and certain southern prefects in March and April 1815 may be found in A.D.H.G., 4M33.

[11] Bibliothèque Thiers, Fonds Masson, Carton 6, Vitrolles to Baron Trouvé, prefect of the Aude, April 1, 1815, has this heading.

cruitment: "We did not think we ought to look too carefully for guarantees of character and morality . . ." [12]

On June 26, the day after Marseilles was liberated, royalists attempted to take over Toulouse. General Decaen, however, unlike his counterpart in Marseilles, refused to yield and suppressed the uprising. All those suspected of having participated were brought before a military tribunal, which thereafter assumed responsibility for punishing seditious acts.[13] A severely repressive regime continued until July 17. Then, a week before Marshal Brune withdrew from Toulon, General Decaen arranged to withdraw his own troops from Toulouse. At that point the *secrets* were mobilized and grouped into four companies, forming a battalion of 600 men.[14]

Toulouse was liberated only nine days after Louis XVIII's return to Paris. Although his Ministry made new appointments to local office, a minimum of five days was required for such decisions to reach Toulouse. When the announcement of new appointments did arrive, an immediate conflict of interests was apparent. Ardent royalists in Toulouse wanted their own candidates, some of whom had spent the preceding months in hiding or exile, to assume public office in the recently liberated areas, even in the face of opposition from Paris. By July 21 two sets of officials confronted one another in a contest for the exercise of civil and military authority in the department. One group had been named by the Paris Ministry and included officeholders of the First Restoration. The other group represented the candidates

---

[12] A.D.H.G., 4M36, Chazelles, subprefect of Muret, to the prefect, Rémusat, September 8, 1815.

[13] A.D. Gard, 4M22, decree of General Decaen, June 28, 1815, establishing the military court. It was sent out to the civil and military authorities in the 9th and 10th military divisions. These included the following departments respectively: Ardèche, Aveyron, Gard, Hérault, Lozère, and Tarn; Ariège, Aude, Haute-Garonne, Gers, Haute-Pyrénées, Pyrénées-Orientales, and Tarn-et-Garonne.

[14] A.D.H.G., 4M36, Chazelles, subprefect of Muret, to the prefect, Rémusat, December 8, 1815.

of Angoulême and the clandestine royalist organization, the Chevaliers de la Foi.

The Chevaliers de la Foi was a secret royalist society organized about 1810 by Ferdinand de Bertier de Sauvigny, youngest son of the late Intendant of Paris.[15] Ferdinand would bring to the organization the zeal for legitimism which the horrible massacre of his father had left as his own personal legacy. Heir in its goals to the Institut Philanthropique which had advanced the royalist cause under the Directory, the society of the Chevaliers was an important instrument during the last year of the Empire in mobilizing public support for a restoration of the Bourbon monarchy. The organization came to develop roots in almost every part of France but, outside of centers like Paris and Toulouse, remained almost exclusively aristocratic in its recruitment. It escaped discovery by modeling itself upon the ritual secrecy of the Masons, by an emphasis on the oral communication of information, and by the creation of a public service "front" organization, the Associés de Charité, from which its membership could be recruited. The strength of the organization in Toulouse was based in part on a royalist sentiment that was manifest during the period of the Directory and was sufficiently strong to motivate an unsuccessful royalist uprising in 1799. The history of Angoulême's liberation movement is closely intertwined with that of the Chevaliers de la Foi.

In the contest for office of mayor of Toulouse at the beginning of the Second Restoration, the candidate of the Paris Ministry confronted a member of the Chevaliers de la Foi. Baron Joseph de Malaret, the Paris candidate, had received his title from Napoleon only the preceding year. He had occupied the office of mayor under the Empire and the First Restoration. Having resigned during the Hundred Days, he expected to be able to return

---

[15] See G. de Bertier, *Le comte Ferdinand de Bertier* (Paris, 1948), especially iii.

to his former position when the Bourbons returned. However, he was prevented from so doing by the local royalist committee, which resented his refusal to cooperate with the Chevaliers de la Foi in their attempt to liberate the city of Toulouse before Wellington's arrival in April 1814. The royalist committee brought in their own candidate and a member of the Chevaliers, Joseph de Villèle, to assume that office.[16]

In the prefectoral contest in Toulouse at the beginning of the Second Restoration, Charles-Antoine de Limayrac, brother-in-law of Joseph de Villèle, and a fellow member of the Chevaliers de la Foi, exercised his authority under mandate from the Duke of Angoulême. He did not immediately relinquish his post when Augustin-Laurent de Rémusat, a candidate of the Paris Ministry, was sworn in on July 21.[17]

An equally important contest occurred over the supervision of military forces in the department. The candidate supported by Paris was General Ramel, who had been commander of the Napoleonic garrison in Toulouse at the end of the Hundred Days. It was on his orders, nevertheless, that the tricolor had been lowered and the white flag of the Bourbons raised in its place. Ramel soon found before him another candidate for his office in Maréchal de Camp Adrien de Rougé. Rougé had been a leader in the royalist insurrection of 1799, and had fought the campaign of April 1815 with Angoulême, following the Duke to Spain.[18]

---

[16] See *ibid.*, p. 137, for Malaret; Villèle describes his advent as mayor of Toulouse in *Mémoires*, I, 301 ff.

[17] For Limayrac's membership in the Chevaliers de la Foi, see F. de Bertier, "Souvenirs," cited in G. de Bertier, *Le comte Ferdinand de Bertier*, p. 137. Rémusat was named to the position of prefect on the suggestion of Talleyrand and Pasquier. He had had a career in the imperial administration, but had resigned during the Hundred Days. See Etienne-Denis de Pasquier, *Histoire de mon temps: Mémoires du Chancelier Pasquier* (Paris, 1894), III, 350; Charles de Rémusat, *Mémoires de ma vie . . . (1797–1820)*, ed. Charles Pouthas (Paris, 1958), I, 215.

[18] A.D.H.G., 4M36, subprefect of Saint-Gaudens to prefect, July 22, 1815, offers an interesting illustration of the confusion created by the contest between Ramel and Rougé.

The dispute over military power in the department was resolved by Marshal Pérignon, Angoulême's special delegate in the Haute-Garonne. A veteran of the campaign of April and the Spanish exile, he had returned to take the place of General Decaen as governor of the tenth military division. In this capacity, he divided the military command in the department between Rougé and Ramel. The former, with whom he had plotted in Spain, was made commander-in-chief of a newly-created royal corps of the department while General Ramel was given command of the national guard and the corps of the regular army, stationed principally in Toulouse.[19] The garrison over which Ramel had charge was, however, of diminishing importance. Desertions had decimated its strength, as the mayor indicated in his register on July 15: "The soldiers who composed the 79th line regiment in garrison at Toulouse have all deserted, so that the corps is almost entirely dissolved." [20] Ramel had to fall back on the national guard to maintain order in the city.

With many more soldiers to rely upon, Maréchal de Camp Rougé's position was stronger. Three main sources made up the royal corps of which he had been made commander. First among those recruited were soldiers deserting from Ramel's garrison in Toulouse. The prefect of the Haute-Garonne mentioned them specifically in his report to the Minister:

Several battalions of royalist volunteers are being formed . . . Soldiers of the line who leave their corps are admitted . . . They receive uniform and pay, and their number is already considerable.[21]

A second source lay in the royalist secret companies which were

---

[19] A.D.H.G., 4M147, Pérignon to Ramel, July 18, 1815.

[20] Registre de correspondance du maire [de Toulouse], IV, July 18, 1815, quoted in Jean Loubet, "Le gouvernement Toulousain du Duc d'Augoulême, après les Cent Jours," La Révolution Française, XIV (1913), 150–151.

[21] A.N., F⁷3786, Bulletin de Police of August 8, 1815, quoting prefectoral report of July 25, 1815.

called up on the day of General Decaen's departure. Only one of
the four companies of the battalion of 600 was fitted out with
weapons and uniforms.[22] Their uniform, green with white epau-
lettes and ornaments, united the colors of Bourbon and Angoulême. Because of their colors they were popularly designated
as *Verdets*. Some of this company had joined the national guard
as individuals; those who did so led a double life, changing uniforms for their separate obligations to Ramel and Rougé. A third
contribution to Rougé's forces came from the regiment of Marie-
Thérèse, formed by the royalist exiles at Figureras, Spain, during
the Hundred Days.[23]

The mobilization of the Verdets on July 17 introduced a reign
of terror in the life of the city. Charles de Rémusat, son of the
newly-appointed prefect, wrote in his memoirs:

They were an independent and secret company, a band of hired
ruffians *(sbires)* commanded by criminal agents *(séides)* exercis-
ing unhampered control. On the slightest pretext, they made arrests or searched houses, in order to put an end to the supposed
intrigues of Bonapartists or *fédérés* . . .[24]

The wife of the prefect summarized the threat very succinctly:
"informers are active, arrests are being made, and a sort of terror
reigns here." [25]

Police files in Toulouse contain a list of almost 500 persons

[22] A.D.H.G., 4M36, Chazelles to Rémusat, September 8, 1815; Registre de
correspondance du maire [de Toulouse], IV, July 18, 1815, cited in J. Loubet,
"Le gouvernement Toulousain du Duc d'Angoulême," p. 157.

[23] Bibliothèque Thiers, Fonds Masson, Carton 6, Baron [Etienne] de Damas-
Crux, Précis des opérations de M. le Lieutenant-général, Comte de Damas-Crux,
n.d. [August? 1815]. Damas was Angoulême's chief of military operations.

[24] Ch. de Rémusat, *Mémoires*, I, 225–226. See a similar description by a contemporary of the activity of the Verdets in E. Connac, "La réaction royaliste à
Toulouse: trois lettres inédites de Picot de Lapeyrouse," *Revue des Pyrénées*, X
(1898), 431–451.

[25] Letter of July 26, 1815 to an undesignated woman in Paris, in Paul de
Rémusat, ed., *Correspondance de M. [Mme.] de Rémusat pendant les premières
années de la Restauration* (Paris, 1883), I, 82.

considered suspect by royalists then in control of the city. The character of the list, and the fact that it was found among the papers of a special police chief appointed by the royalist committee, indicate the radical effort in progress to root out the leadership and sympathizers of earlier regimes and avenge wounds of the past. The catalog of complaints against individual suspects runs the span of revolutionary and Bonapartist activities:

Former president of the *société populaire* . . . stubborn Jacobin propagandist; outspoken Republican . . . extreme revolutionary, member of the secret club . . . infamous regicide, has signed the pact of federation . . . exploited his master at the time of the emigration . . . one of the most dedicated members of the revolutionary tribunal; informer in 1793 [etc.] [26]

Many who were not suspect for their revolutionary past were under suspicion for having joined clubs of Bonapartists organized during the Hundred Days. Affiliation with these *fédérations,* however, had not been a purely personal decision or for that matter a voluntary one. Napoleon's government had supported them actively, and in the South had tried to bring pressure to join on both the purchasers of nationalized properties and public officeholders. Joining the clubs, grouped in a Confédération du Midi, had been presented as a necessary patriotic act.[27]

The political character of the arrests made in July and August was confirmed in an inventory of prisoners made by Savy-Gardeilh, Angoulême's appointee as police commissioner. This statement was drawn up for communication to the moderate prefect of the Haute-Garonne, Rémusat.[28] According to Savy-Gardeilh's

[26] A.D.H.G., 4M35, n.d. [August? 1815], Etat pour faire suite aux précédens de tous les individus qui étaient conjurés avant l'incursion de Bonaparte.

[27] A.D.H.G., 4M34, Minister of Police to prefect of the Haute-Garonne, June 7, 1815, and copy of letter to subprefects repeating the appeal to join the confederation.

[28] A.D.H.G., 4M35, Etat des détenus . . . commissaire général de police to prefect, August 14, 1815. Savy-Gardeilh took the responsibility for these arrests.

report in mid-August a total of only 35 persons were being held in custody. His comments on the persons involved indicated that almost all were being held for political offenses. He noted only one arrest for theft and three for assassination attempts. With the exception of these four the arrests had been made for political acts, associations, and ideas. However, the number of persons in prison as political suspects was undoubtedly larger than this report indicated. Savy-Gardeilh had every reason to want to minimize to outsiders the number of persons affected by the local royalist reaction. His loyalties lay with the secret companies of which his son was a member.[29] He himself had fought the campaign of April with Angoulême, and followed him to Spain.[30]

Rémusat was not deceived by Savy-Gardeilh's statement, and his earlier reports to the Ministry of Police in Paris set the figure of those arrested much higher than thirty-five. Although Rémusat's first report on local conditions, sent out on July 25, simply spoke of many arrests of men designated as *fédérés*,[31] a subsequent report on August 4 set the figure of those arrested at about 100. The prefect reported that some 40 of those detained had been freed and that others would be liberated as information was gathered about them.[32]

In fact, Rémusat did put pressure on Villèle, the mayor of Toulouse, to assure the protection of the courts to those arrested. For those against whom charges could be preferred he asked that arrangements be made for hearings. Villèle hedged his response,

[29] A.D.H.G., wU620. The membership of his son in the secret companies is affirmed by several persons testifying about a crime in which the son was implicated.

[30] A.N., F1cIII, Haute-Garonne, information on eligible electors, August 1815, describes both Savy-Gardeilh and his son as men who fought with Angoulême in April, and followed him into exile.

[31] A.N., F73786, Bulletin de Police, August 8, 1815. The report took unusually long to reach Paris. Five to six days was the usual time required. Reports from Toulouse were usually summarized in the bulletin a week after they had been dispatched.

[32] A.N., F73786, Bulletins de Police, August 9 and August 11, 1815.

refusing to acknowledge responsibility for arrests made without
the sanction of duly authorized persons:

I cannot answer for the arrests made outside the limits of this
commune by other authorities, but I can assure you that all persons arrested by order of the city government will be freed in
twenty-four hours or arraigned before you or the courts.[33]

Villèle was later revealed to be a great deal more knowledgeable
about the activities of private royalist groups making arrests in
the city than he chose to indicate at this time. The lid was to be
lifted on the royalist conspiracy by revelations made after the
assassination of General Ramel.

General Jean-Pierre Ramel had had a very checkered political
career. In his early twenties, at the outbreak of the war against
the First Coalition, he had abandoned his position as an officer
in the national guard at Cahors to join the Republican army. For
a brief period thereafter he rose rapidly within the ranks. However, he had been selected to defend the Corps Législatif against
Napoleon's coup d'état of Fructidor and found himself, as a result, one of the first to be proscribed under the Consulate. Unwilling to vanish from the public scene, he made a dramatic
escape from his prison in Cayenne and returned to France. Napoleon pardoned him and he rejoined the French Army in the
Iberian campaign. At the First Restoration Louis XVIII raised
him to the rank of Maréchal de Camp although hesitating to
place him on active duty. Napoleon maintained Ramel's rank
during the Hundred Days and made him garrison commander
in Toulouse. After Waterloo he retained his rank and his command.

As garrison commander of Toulouse with control over the national guard Ramel had authority to interfere with the activities

[33] A.D.H.G., 4M35, August 22, 1815.

of the secret companies. A contest between Ramel and the secret companies developed in early August. The latter saw that certain private subsidies previously provided for them were no longer as regular or as adequate as they had been and feared that their units would soon be dissolved. The men of these companies came to Ramel often in early August asking to draw pay and uniforms from the funds of the national guard. Ramel was firm in refusing to incorporate them as a unit but he did offer to integrate them as individuals. His intention was to divide them up among separate companies and not to allow them a common identity or command. The last time Ramel received representatives of these companies was on August 14; he gave them the same answer he had given two or three times before. They were not satisfied.[34]

Celebrations after the liberation of the city had continued into August, exaggerating the movement of the throngs gathering nightly in the streets. On Assumption Day, August 15, movement in the streets was particularly intense. The previous day had seen the meeting of the electoral college of the district. Malaret, mayor during the Hundred Days, and choice of the Paris Ministry for the presidency of the electoral college, had yielded to threats and left the city beforehand. General Ramel, who had been president of the electoral college during the Hundred Days, had been threatened with death unless he too left town. He refused, and on the night of August 15 was enjoying a leisurely dinner with friends.

Ramel was called from the dinner table by the news that a hostile crowd was forming in front of his lodgings in the Place des Carmes. He immediately mounted and proceeded to the square, followed by an aide. Once there he found it difficult to move. Members of the crowd, which included at least 50 Verdets, surged against him and tried to unhorse him. Ramel called on

---

[34] Prefect Rémusat felt that this dispute was of prime importance in explaining the later attempt on Ramel's life. See A.N., F⁷6829, Dr. 3012, prefect to Minister, August 17, 1815.

the captain of the national guard present at the time to do his duty, and then drew his own sword. He was shot in the stomach after wounding a few of the Verdets with his swinging saber. Although the captain of the guards rushed to help him, no unit was available to disperse the crowd. Not until later that evening did Angoulême's appointees, Mayor Villèle and Marshal Pérignon, appear in the square. The latter dispersed the crowd with the aid of royalist companies under his command and then retired.

Ramel, meanwhile, had tried to get to his residence but found the door barricaded from the inside. Friends entered from a side street to open the door for him and carried him up to his room. The crowd had still not been dispersed and two intruders reached his room while his friends were out searching for a doctor. They left his body one open wound.[35]

The justices of the peace did not come to take Ramel's testimony until the second day after the assault. Ramel then stated that he could not identify the men who had committed the injuries but that Savy-Gardeilh and Rigaud were the men responsible. On the evening of that day, August 17, General Ramel died. Royalists in the city tried to create the impression that Ramel had attacked the Verdets first, in ostensible proof of which some members went about the square afterwards showing their saber wounds. Testimony was collected in the month that followed, but in September 1815 the case appeared to be closed with the indictment of three individuals *in absentia*.[36]

It was not until September of the following year that the case was reopened. At that time the government in Paris feared that without a show of ministerial authority in Toulouse the elections in the department to the Chamber of Deputies would turn against the moderate ministerial candidates as they had the pre-

[35] See A.D.H.G., wU620, wU621. Two volumes of testimony in the judicial inquiry present a rather full description of the circumstances of the crime, though not of the specific individuals responsible.

[36] "Un chapitre inconnu de l'affaire Ramel," *Revue historique de Toulouse,* XXIII (1936), 225–237; Armand Praviel, "Le massacre de Ramel," *Oeuvres Libres* (Paris, 1927), LXXVIII, 269–320.

vious August. Responsibility for the new investigation was given to Combettes-Caumont, counselor in the *cour royale,* and descended from a line of magistrates of the Parlement of Toulouse. Though an aristocrat and royalist in sentiment, he had married the daughter of a regicide of the Convention and for this reason was kept out of the inner royalist circle in Toulouse. Living in the "fief" of the Chevaliers de la Foi, he had not been admitted to membership in the secret society.[37]

From October 1816 to March 1817 Combettes-Caumont conducted an investigation in which over 300 persons were questioned and as a result of which 18 arrests were made. Ten accused persons were sent before the provost court on March 4, 1817, but this number was later reduced to six. Three of the six escaped and the Minister of Justice intervened through the Court of Cassation to have the case transferred to the provost court in Pau where the magistrates would be less subject to local pressures. The trial in Pau opened on April 5, 1817 with Combettes-Caumont presenting the case for the state. The judgment delivered on August 26, 1817 affected the three accused persons present for the trial: one was acquitted and the other two condemned to short terms of forced labor. In an extraordinary move the following day the three accused persons in flight were acquitted.[38]

Despite the unsatisfactory outcome of the trial from the state's point of view, Combettes-Caumont's inquiry had established certain unusual facts about the circumstances of the killing and his investigation had yielded important information about the organization and aims of certain ultra-royalists in Toulouse. At the trial Combettes-Caumont had argued that the assassination of General Ramel had been planned, and that certain circumstances connected with the crime suggested the complicity of city officials. First, the crowd had not been immediately dispersed by the armed units which had gathered at the scene. These included men

---

[37] G. de Bertier, *Le comte Ferdinand de Bertier,* p. 272.
[38] A. de Praviel, "Le massacre de Ramel," pp. 312 ff.

from the national guard and the Marie-Thérèse battalion, who together represented a force of 500 men. Combettes-Caumont argued that the first shot might not have been fatal had the crowd been dispersed so that further harm could not come to the general. A second fact exciting suspicion was that the mayor, Villèle, did not arrive on the scene until a few hours after the crime although his residence was not far away. Third, depositions were not taken by judicial officers immediately after the crime and one of the names given by Ramel appeared to have been inscribed incorrectly in the record of his testimony.[39]

Combettes-Caumont did not reveal at the trial information he had received about the royalist committee responsible for the assassination. Prior to February 1817 he had been having little success in getting information from his 300 witnesses. During that month, however, through the testimony of a well-informed participant, he learned a great deal more about the reasons for the murder.[40]

The new information was supplied by Commère, described as "the only one of those accused who comes from the ordinary mass of the common people and artisans."[41] He was a member of a royalist committee which he described as responsible for the assassination.[42] The executors of the plan, according to Commère,

[39] Combette-Caumont [sic], "Assassinat du Général Ramel, 15 août, 1815," *Mémoires de Tours* (Paris, 1837), III, 227–280.

[40] A.N., BB[30]254. This dossier was first cited by G. de Bertier, *Le comte Ferdinand de Bertier*, p. 272 (footnote 2), and parts were quoted. L. Sancti, "Notes et documents sur les intrigues royalistes dans le Midi de la France de 1792 à 1815," *Mémoires de l'Académie des Sciences de Toulouse*, IV (1916), 90, thought that such documents had been destroyed in 1871.

[41] A.N., BB[30]254, Combettes-Caumont to Minister of Justice, February 13, 1817.

[42] A.N., BB[30]254, report of Combettes-Caumont to Minister of Justice, n.d. [February 1817] lists a de Commère on the royalist committee. It is assumed here that Commère and de Commère are one and the same individual: the kind of information the witness discloses suggests he was a member of that committee. Moreover, the fact that he was "the only one of those accused who comes from the ordinary mass of the common people" allows one to understand why the *particule,* intended for the other names in the series, might have been left erroneously in front of Commère's name. However, see G. de Bertier, *Le comte Ferdinand de Bertier*, pp. 273, 275, where the witness' name is transcribed as Commène, and no connection is made with de Commère.

were de Caldaguès, de Rigaud, and de Savy-Gardeilh, son of the chief of police in Toulouse; the latter two had been implicated by Ramel on his death-bed. The committee which Commère alleged had had the ultimate responsibility for the murder of Ramel had included the most illustrious figures in the Catholic aristocracy of the Southwest: MacCarthy, Raymond, and Damas among others. There is little doubt that this committee was the *bannière*, the local cell, of the Chevaliers de la Foi in Toulouse.[43]

The company of Verdets was described in this testimony as the nucleus of a vast network of secret societies in the department, all at the service of the royalist committee.

The executive power and the agents of this royalist committee were first the secret companies composed of 500 to 600 persons, but little by little these corps increased in numbers. The membership in these secret societies became so considerable that the number was thought to reach 14,000 to 15,000, of which about 1,200 were in the city and the rest spread over the department and surrounding areas.[44]

There was no doubt of the complicity of the Verdets in the murder of Ramel. They had left an inn en masse to converge on the Place des Carmes when informed that Ramel would be there. About 50 of them mixed with the milling crowd in the huge square. Among the 50, Commère testified, only a few were aware of the committee's plan to commit murder. The rest were presumably trying to force Ramel's departure by protest and pressure as had been done in the case of the former mayor, Malaret.

The motive of the murder, according to the witness, arose from the power struggle in progress between the moderate appointees

[43] Nevertheless, Villèle's name was not mentioned by Commère, and Villèle and his biographer deny that he had any responsibility for the murder. See Jean Fourcassié, *Villèle* (Paris, 1954), pp. 75–76.

[44] A.N., BB³⁰254, report of Combettes-Caumont to Minister of Justice, n.d. [February 1817].

of the King, and the officials named by Angoulême in July. The King, on July 18, issued a decree ending the powers of special delegates and revoking their appointments.[45] Angoulême, however, on July 20, ordered his civil and military appointees to remain at their posts,[46] despite the conflict this brought on with rival candidates named by the Ministry in Paris. The King's decree did not arrive in Toulouse until July 25 and a week after the edict arrived Angoulême left for Paris still apparently determined to defend the tenure of his appointees. Nevertheless, after a few days of conversations, he was obliged by the failure of his talks to suspend those appointees.[47]

The royalist committee in Toulouse had decided while Angoulême was in Paris, and without his knowledge, to involve "the people" in their cause. A situation was to be contrived in which the mass of the common people of Toulouse would demonstrate their opposition to moderate royal appointees. On this occasion they were to be made participants in a massacre. According to Commère, it was decided to select for the purpose a moderate royalist who had held office during the Hundred Days, and General Ramel was singled out. The royalist committee, pessimistic about being able to maintain its candidates in office through conversations at the highest level, chose to eliminate the moderate contenders by force. In so doing they were trying to make a conspiratorial minority appear to represent the wishes of the city.

Angoulême's unwillingness to allow candidates of the government in Paris to take office in Languedoc and Provence was, at the least, an attempt to push the government in Paris to the right. However, statements of two members of the royalist committee,

---

[45] E.-D. de Pasquier, *Histoire de mon temps,* III, 360, claimed this was directed against Angoulême.

[46] A.N., F$^{1b}$II, Haute-Garonne 7, ordinance of July 20, 1815, cited in G. de Bertier, *Le comte Ferdinand de Bertier,* p. 176.

[47] See Archives Communales de Toulouse, D$^2$6, cited in J. Loubet, "Le gouvernement Toulousain du Duc d'Angoulême après les Cent Jours," *La Révolution Française,* XIV (1913), 351, for proclamation of August 7. It was later printed in *Le Moniteur* of August 25.

Commère and de Caldaguès, confirmed further plans to establish a separate government in the Midi, a "Kingdom of Aquitaine." [48] One aim of the separatist movement was to oblige the government to oust its imperial personnel still occupying ministerial positions. The removal of men like Fouché and Talleyrand was set as a precondition for dissolving the separatist government. Communications between Ferdinand de Bertier and the Duke de Damas, both Chevaliers de la Foi, and the latter close to Angoulême, confirmed this intention.[49] They also indicated that the royalist movement had a second goal: to limit the Prussian zone of occupation. It was hoped that by joint action of the Midi and the West the Prussians, the most disliked of the foreign occupiers, could be kept from extending their zone of occupation into the Vendée. The mixture of interests, principles, and pure fantasy in the movement was well described by Charles de Rémusat, son of the prefect:

This control over offices was at bottom their first interest but the interest of their party followed closely. More readily avowed and better received, it was colored by two circumstances: the state of northern France, invaded and mistreated by the foreigner; and the situation of Paris, where influences suspect to any royalist dominated the King's policies and circumscribed his freedom. Was it not serving the dynasty, and authority itself, to organize without the King's knowing participation or rather, without the influence of the odious ministers imposed on him, a whole "France du Midi," truly monarchical, at last under the white flag enhanced by the green, a *Royaume d'Occitanie*? These words were pronounced from the first moment [of the

---

[48] According to L. Sancti, "Notes et documents sur les intrigues royalistes," pp. 87–90, Combettes-Caumont received news of this conspiracy from de Caldaguès. From Combettes-Caumont, it was passed to Lamothe-Langon, where it appeared in his *Mémoires d'une femme de qualité,* and to Combettes-Caumont's friend, d'Aldéguier, whose *Histoire de Toulouse,* IV, told of the separatist plans.

[49] F. de Bertier, "Souvenirs," quoted in G. de Bertier, *Le comte Ferdinand de Bertier,* pp. 177–178.

Second Restoration] and these ideas were vaguely present in many minds.[50]

However, after the suspension of Angoulême's appointees and the election of deputies to the new legislature, regionalism, even as a tactic, ceased to have much popularity in the Southwest. Paradoxically, Villèle, the mayor of Toulouse, who had earlier represented the provincial nobility in his hostility to centralized institutions, became a spokesman for effective centralized government. Villèle had spoken for many royalists in Languedoc when, the year before, he had opposed the Charter of 1814.[51] He had agreed that the authority of the King should be limited but not by an assembly elected on the basis of a property franchise. At that time Villèle favored, instead, the re-establishment for this purpose of certain political institutions of the Old Regime, particularly the provincial estates. Angoulême, despite his secessionist tactics at the beginning of the Second Restoration, was fundamentally committed a year earlier to the centralization of state power.

In Villèle's view the Duke had accepted during his long residence abroad the foreigner's uncritical admiration for Napoleon's achievements in centralized administration.[52] An incident reported in Villèle's memoirs is significant for what it illustrated of their earlier differences. The Duke had re-entered Languedoc in the spring of 1814; local authorities were showing him the monuments and public works. One official remarked with pride and regret, "our Estates were responsible for these projects." The Duke's reply was awaited with interest. Villèle reported that those gathered about him were astonished to hear Angoulême

<hr />

[50] C. de Rémusat, *Mémoires de ma vie,* I, 214–215.

[51] J. de Villèle, "Observations sur le projet de Constitution," May 20, 1814, reprinted in J. de Villèle, *Mémoires,* I, 499–509. See also pp. 254–263 for his objections to the property franchise.

[52] J. de Villèle, *Mémoires,* I, 222.

say rather sternly, "We prefer the departments to the provinces." [53]

The legislative elections of August 1815 carried Joseph de Villèle to Paris as a deputy from the Haute-Garonne. Along with him went Charles-Antoine de Limayrac to the Chamber of Deputies and Robert MacCarthy to the Chamber of Peers. All were members of the Chevaliers de la Foi, which had swept the elections in the Midi. The Chevaliers de la Foi now exercised a controlling voice in the Chamber of Deputies. [54] Their theories on the organization of state power changed with their new role. They no longer opposed the authority of the central government but tried to make it reflect their own viewpoint. In so doing they participated in the second phase of the reaction—a legal Terror, effected from Paris through legislative action and ministerial decree. Before this phase was entered on, however, public attention was drawn to Bas Languedoc where the political reaction in the Gard assumed the guise of religious persecution.

[53] *Ibid.*, p. 248. For a recent bibliography on proposals for the decentralization of government under the Restoration, see Alan Spitzer, "The Bureaucrat as Proconsul: The Restoration Prefect and the Police Générale," *Comparative Studies in Society and History*, VII (The Hague, 1965), 371–372.

[54] See G. de Bertier, *Le comte Ferdinand de Bertier*, p. 190.

# III

# THE REACTION IN THE GARD

At the close of the Empire, one third the membership of the Reformed Church in France remained settled in the territory of Bas Languedoc and the Hautes- and Basses-Cévennes. At the heart of this concentration of 150,000 to 200,000 Calvinists was the Gard; other centers of Protestant population could be found in adjacent areas of the departments of the Hérault and the Lozère.[1]

The heaviest urban concentration of Calvinists in this region was in Nîmes, capital of the Gard. With its 14,000 communicants, one out of every three citizens, Nîmes ranked second only to Paris as a center of Calvinist strength. Exceptional in numbers, the Protestants of Nîmes were also exceptional in wealth. Though constituting but a third of the city's population, they controlled its commerce and industry[2] and had made Nîmes the wealthiest

[1] André Siegfried, "Le groupe Protestant Cévenol sous la IIIe République," in Marc Boegner et al., *Protestantisme français* (Paris, 1945), p. 208, has called this region "the fortress" of French Protestantism. Daniel Robert, *Les Eglises Réformées en France (1800–1830)* (Paris, 1961), pp. 4–5, 12, establishes its population in 1815. Reformed Church refers to the membership of the Calvinist Consistories.

[2] See A.N., F⁷9049, extract of report of *inspecteur de la gendarmerie* of the Gard, enclosed with letter of Minister of War to Minister of Police, November 7, 1815. This source estimated Protestants held two thirds of the commercial and industrial enterprises in Nîmes, employing 12,000 to 13,000 persons. For a study of the Protestant community in Montauban in the seventeen-eighties, see Daniel Ligou, "La structure sociale du Protestantisme Montalbanais à la fin du XVIIIe siècle," *Bulletin de la Société de l'histoire du Protestantisme français,* C (1954), pp. 93–110. No comparable study of the Protestant role in Nîmes' economic life has been undertaken.

center of Calvinism in France.[3] The heavy mixing of Protestants with Catholics in Nîmes was unusual for the Gard. Elsewhere in the department the two groups had generally settled in geographically distinct areas. Protestants lived in the north and the west, in the historic shelter of the Cévennes mountains. The southern and eastern sections of the department, running along the Rhône to the sea, were part of a largely Catholic belt.

Protestants had benefited enormously from both the legislation and the executive decrees of the revolutionary and Napoleonic regimes.[4] From them had come freedom of public worship, access to municipal and judicial office, and expanded economic opportunities. These had meant the final end of a period of "second-class" citizenship which dated from the revocation of the Edict of Nantes. Emancipation had, in fact, begun at the end of the Old Regime, leaving the remaining inequalities all the more unacceptable. In 1787 a royal edict had legalized Protestant marriages and property transfers, restoring legal status to the Protestant family. The royal convocation on January 24, 1789 mentioned no religious qualification for the second and third estates and that year French Protestants participated in elections for the States-General. However, restrictions on Protestant eligibility for office in the magistrature, the municipalities, and the universities remained and neither decree had restored freedom of worship.

At the beginning of the Revolution members of the Protestant bourgeoisie, in Nîmes as in Montauban, had profited from their new eligibility for public office by assuming positions in the municipal administration and the national guard. They held those

[3] See the rank list by wealth of Calvinist communities in D. Robert, *Les Eglises Réformées,* p. 13. After Nîmes, there followed: (1) Lyons, Marseilles, Bordeaux, La Rochelle, Montpellier; (2) Montauban, Castres, Nantes, Rouen, Caen, and Sedan; (3) Uzès, Alès, Sète, Anduze, St.-Hyppolyte, Orléans, and Ganges.

[4] See Burdette Poland, *French Protestants and the French Revolution* (Princeton, 1957), esp. pp. 81 ff. for a summary.

posts until the Girondists fell from power. When, during the Terror of 1793–94, the revolutionary tribunal turned against the Girondists, the Protestant community suffered the heaviest losses.[5] After Thermidor the Calvinist bourgeoisie resumed a position of political influence. This was maintained under the Directory and Consulate.

Under the Empire Protestants tended to control the mayor's office in Nîmes, the municipal council, and a majority of posts in the municipal administration. While the highest positions in the district courts and the appeals court went to Catholics, Protestants were numerous among the lesser magistrates. In the departmental administration, however, their participation was limited to representation on the departmental council. The prefects and almost all the subprefects were Catholic throughout the Empire.[6]

This period of relative political strength had been used to improve the position of the Protestant Consistory in Nîmes. First, the Protestants acquired houses of worship within the city. They took advantage of the sale of ecclesiastical properties to purchase a church that had belonged to a Dominican order and to lease from a Protestant buyer the chapel of a former Ursuline convent. These were used by the Consistory throughout the Empire.[7] Secondly, profiting from certain clauses of the Concordat of 1801, they successfully protested against the right of the Catholic majority to hold religious processions in the streets of Nîmes. Nîmes

[5] Clement Perrot, "Report on the Persecutions of the French Protestants" (London, 1816), ms. in Bibliothèque du Protestantisme Français, 3209. Anon., *Défense des Protestants du Bas-Languedoc* (1815), p. 4.

[6] A.N., F⁷9049, Eymard to Minister of Police, November 29, 1815. Eymard was a well-regarded investigator for the Haute Police. He had held a prefect's post in Provence. A collection of his reports may be found scattered in the F⁷ series, as well as in a collection at the Archives Privées.

[7] D. Robert, *Les Eglises Réformées*, pp. 281, 609 (Annexe IV: Temples). The Reformed Church in France had acquired 100 churches under the Consulate and the Empire: *ibid.*, pp. 123–125.

43

became the only major city south of the Loire to secure this prohibition.[8] Such acts had produced some tension locally but relations between the two communities were good at the end of the Empire.[9]

At the First Restoration the Consistory of Nîmes declared its royalism and requested the distinguishing external signs. In July of 1814 the president of the Consistory sought the royalist decoration of the fleur-de-lys for 27 pastors and lay members of the Protestant community in Nîmes. The prefect awarded these to the Consistory in October.[10] The president of the Consistory also used his influence to bring pastors elsewhere to a benevolent attitude toward the new regime. When informants in the Ministry of the Interior announced to him that a pastor in Caen was suspect for his political ideas, the president of the Consistory in Nîmes suggested to the pastor that he make his royalism clear from the pulpit:

It is she [the House of Bourbon] who has given you the Edict of 1787. It is Louis XVIII who has procured peace and the constitutional charter. It is the King who can alone shelter us from the evil intentions of our enemies and allow us the enjoyment of our civil and religious liberty.[11]

The Bourbons were evidently satisfied with the loyalty of the Protestant community in the Gard during the First Restoration.

[8] *Ibid.*, pp. 97–98. Other principal cities in which processions were forbidden were Paris, Strasbourg, Mulhouse, and probably Colmar. Article 45 of the Concordat of 1801 was understood to prohibit street processions in cities where a Consistory opposed them.

[9] On this subject, see, for example, Archives Privées, Papiers Eymard, Eymard to Decazes (manuscript notes), August 13, 1814; F.O. 27/130, Report by Ross, January 21, 1816. Ross was investigating the situation in southern France for the British Foreign Office.

[10] Arch. Cons. Nîmes, B53[23], Chabaud to President of Consistory, July 18, 1814; B53[5], Prefect Rolland (Gard) to President of Consistory, October 25, 1814.

[11] Arch. Cons. Nîmes, B53[6], copy of letter from President of Consistory in Nîmes to pastor in Caen, February 24, 1815.

There were no great purges at that time and the administration of the late Empire remained in office throughout the First Restoration. The prefect, Jean-Louis-Antoine de Rolland, nominated in 1810, retained his position until April 1815. With him stayed the subprefects and all but one of the municipal mayors named by the Emperor. The one new appointee was the Baron de Daunant, sworn in as mayor of Nîmes in July 1814.[12] The Protestant succession in the mayor's office in Nîmes was maintained.

Napoleon's return from Elba, however, brought a change in the position of Protestants in the Gard. The appearance of the Duke of Angoulême in the department, to rally volunteers to fight against Napoleon's troops, marked the first stage in a widening gulf between the two communities. Among the 2,000 royalist volunteers sent from Nîmes to Lyons between March 22 and March 29, 1815, there were only six to ten Protestants.[13] Protestants at the time claimed they were not allowed to join.[14] However, throughout Bas Languedoc, in those districts where the Protestants predominated, there were few volunteers for the defense of the monarchy. The prefect of the neighboring department of the Aveyron confirmed this fact in a report at the end of March 1815:

The volunteers that I called up in the capital of the department yesterday did not show up, and although the mass of the population is well intentioned, I cannot count on any energetic support from them. My position . . . is not very satisfactory, especially in the districts of Millau and Saint-Affrique, because of the large number of Protestants and the fact that many individuals have already displayed the tricolor.[15]

[12] A.N., F⁷9657, Prefect Rolland (Gard) to Minister, April 13, 1815.
[13] P. L. Baragnon, *Abrégé de l'histoire de Nismes* (Nismes, 1835), IV, 217–218, gives the names of six.
[14] *Défense des Protestants du Bas-Languedoc* (1815), pp. 7 ff.; Lauze de Peret, *Causes et précis des troubles en 1815 et 1816* (Paris, 1819), pp. 13–14, 37, 296.
[15] A.D.H.G., 4M33, prefect of Aveyron to Vitrolles, March 29, 1815.

The dissolution of the royalist army on April 9 took place under circumstances that further compromised the Protestant community in the Gard. In small units, the royalist volunteers, dispersed below Lyons, made their way through the Cévennes to destinations in southern and southwestern France. They tried to keep to the back roads and to avoid centers of population, for traffic on the major roads was controlled by Napoleon, and the volunteers were unlawfully armed. At Arpaillargues, a small Protestant commune near Uzès in the Gard, a detachment of volunteers was attacked by a suspicious peasantry armed with pitchforks and clubs; 12 to 15 royalists were killed.[16] The circumstances of the attack left some doubt about the responsibility for the bloodshed. Nevertheless, after the incident, Catholic royalists in the department felt that an account had to be settled with the Protestant community.

When the Emperor regained control over Nîmes, he replaced the prefect and brought the civil administration in the Gard increasingly into the hands of the military. General Gilly was given command of the troops stationed in the department and appointive powers over the police.[17] Few changes, however, were made in the city government of Nîmes. Mayor Daunant remained at his post as did the members of the municipal council. The returning royalist volunteers found the city government, hardly changed in its composition, supporting Napoleon. Furthermore, the national guard had been purged of its royalists[18] and was now closed to them. A few of the royalist volunteers were shot at the gates of the city and many molested within its walls.[19] According to a decree issued by Bonaparte, the higher officers of

---

[16] F.O. 27/130, report of Ross, January 11, 1816, found that more than 15 were killed. Lauze de Peret, *Causes et précis,* p. 13, argues that there were only two dead.

[17] A.D. Gard, 6M22, Minister of Police to prefect, June 20, 1815.

[18] R. de Bernis, *Précis de ce qui s'est passé en 1815 dans les départemens du Gard et de la Lozère* (Paris and Nîmes, 1818), pp. 38–39.

[19] A.N., BB⁶373, procureur-général to Minister of Justice, July 29, 1816.

Angoulême's army were to be placed under surveillance and the rest were to be recruited into the army. Some, seeking to evade the new conscription edict, took refuge in the surrounding countryside.[20]

During the Hundred Days, there was intense political activity on the part of both royalist and Bonapartist secret societies. Membership in these societies reflected the confessional dividing lines in politics. The only royalist secret association in Nîmes which private and official reports identified by name was known as the *Société de Balse*.[21] It emerged during the Hundred Days, and was active through at least the first two years of the Second Restoration. Supporters of the Empire met in the federations, which were widely supported by Protestants. One café, which took the name "Ile d'Elbe," was reported during the Hundred Days as the meeting-place of a secret Bonapartist society.[22]

The ultra-royalist secret societies in the department were part of the network established in the last two years of the Empire. A reliable contemporary description of their aims and activity suggests that they were linked to the Chevaliers de la Foi:

Near the end of 1813, some individuals devoted to the King established in the area encompassed by Nîmes, Arles, Marseilles, St.-Gilles, and Remoulin, societies whose aim was to hasten the recall of the royal family to France, by accelerating the collapse of Bonaparte . . . [To their activity] must be attributed the extraordinary enthusiasm that Catholics showed through this region in learning of the events of early April [1814].[23]

Nîmes found itself menaced by royalist forces shortly after the evacuation of Marseilles. The pressure to oust General Gilly and

[20] R. de Bernis, *Précis,* pp. 15–16.
[21] *Ibid.,* p. 7.
[22] C. Durand, *Marseille, Nismes et ses environs en 1815* (Paris, 1818), part III, 18.
[23] Archives Privées, Papiers Eymard, Eymard to Decazes, September 1, 1814.

his garrison from Nîmes was generated in Provence. A first appeal came from the Royalist Committee of Marseilles, shortly after they had assumed control over that city. Their proclamation on June 26, 1815, sent to the mayor of Nîmes, asked for support. Threatening that "Provence and the entire Midi will become a new Vendée if necessary," they announced the impending collapse of Napoleon's government, and the danger of civil war.[24] Solidly Catholic Beaucaire, in the southeastern part of the Gard, had just passed into the hands of the royalists. From Beaucaire there came a second warning on July 3, in a proclamation by two delegates of Angoulême. René de Bernis and Jules de Calvière asked the residents of the Gard to abandon "a criminal cause" and follow royalist instructions. New appointments to high civil and military posts were announced and all public officeholders named by the Emperor were told to relinquish their positions.[25]

General Gilly did not immediately yield to this insistence but began negotiations with the new civil and military authorities in Beaucaire. On July 6 an agreement was reached in which both sides consented to cease further military action until news was received from Paris about Napoleon's successor.[26] To reduce further the chance of civil strife the municipal council of Nîmes undertook its own negotiations with the royalist authorities in Beaucaire.[27] Gilly, however, so misread the course of events outside the department that, like Marshal Brune in Toulon, he followed the news of Napoleon's abdication with the proclamation of his son, Napoleon II, as successor.

News of the King's arrival in Paris on July 8 reached Nîmes on July 15. The following day, Gilly withdrew; with him were

[24] A.N., F⁷9049, comité royal provisoire to mayor of Nîmes, June 27, 1815.

[25] The text of this proclamation may be found in R. de Bernis, *Précis,* pp. 31 ff. It is quoted in part in Lauze de Peret, *Causes et précis,* pp. 151–52.

[26] A.D. Gard, 6M22, agreement of July 6, 1815. See Extrait du registre du conseil municipal de Nîmes, July 7, 1815, for the proclamation.

[27] A.D. Gard, 6M22, Extrait du registre du conseil municipal de Nîmes, July 7, 1815.

500 men from his garrison, and almost as many members of national guard units from surrounding Cévenol villages. The rest of the garrison was due to evacuate the following day.[28] A dispute arose, however, over the surrender of the artillery and members of the national guard of Nîmes barricaded themselves in with the remaining troops while arguing the terms of the surrender. They were fired upon and eventually disarmed by the disorderly royalist forces who had made their way from Beaucaire.[29] These forces were composed of the national guard of Beaucaire, deserters and vagabonds organized with veterans of the April campaign, and trained military chiefs under Angoulême's command. After they had entered the city a reign of terror began.

On the night of July 17 the officials designated by Angoulême's delegates in the proclamation of July 3 assumed office. General Jean de Barre, who had been made commander of military forces in the department, had no rivals for that office. Vidal, who had been appointed a special police commissioner in the Gard, assumed an office newly-created and therefore uncontested. Only Jules de Calvière, named prefect of the Gard by Angoulême, found that the functions which he was to assume were contested by another.

His rival for the office, Joseph d'Arbaud-Joucques, named by the Ministry in Paris to the post of prefect, arrived in Nîmes on July 28. Before his arrival, however, Angoulême's delegate, Bernis, had appointed new subprefects in all four districts and new mayors throughout the department.[30] In the presence of Angoulême's appointees Arbaud-Joucques was unable to carry out his responsibilities. He wrote letters to both Angoulême in Toulouse

---

[28] Compare the figures in A.N., F⁷9657, Bernis to Minister of Interior, July 19, 1815, and R. de Bernis, *Précis,* p. 36. Regular troops in Gilly's garrison must have numbered about 1,000.

[29] C. Durand, *Marseille, Nismes et ses environs,* p. 52, offers a spectator's graphic account of the appearance of these royalist troops.

[30] A.N., F⁷9657, Bernis to Minister, July 19, 1815.

and his own Minister in Paris in the hope that the contending authorities would clarify his situation. Before Paris could respond, members of the government of the Midi which Angoulême had established in Toulouse requested him to appear personally before them.[31] On July 31, Arbaud-Joucques left for Toulouse. He did not return to his post until August 16.[32]

During his absence the uncontrolled ravages of the royalist bands that had entered Nîmes continued without abatement. No force could be brought to oppose them; the garrison had been evacuated, and the national guard reorganized. Purged of its bourgeois and Protestant members it had been opened first to royalist volunteers of the preceding March and April. Only four Protestants, who had served with Angoulême, were allowed to enter.[33] In its new form, with property qualifications for membership removed, the national guard could not be expected to oppose the royalist bands.

When these bands entered Nîmes they already had a record of property destruction and extortion carried out in their march from Beaucaire. Rich country houses on the outskirts of the city had been destroyed or sacked and wealthy citizens put to ransom.[34] The bands had also struck at the many Protestant artisans whose homes were small workshops of the silk industry. According to an English observer: "The greater part of the houses pillaged belonged to the poor, whose stocking and silk frames the depradators broke, and thus they remain destitute of the means of subsistence."[35] Outside of Nîmes the destruction extended to farm buildings and to the crops themselves.[36]

---

[31] A.N., F⁷9657, Arbaud-Joucques to Minister, July 31, 1815; A.N., F⁷9657, Angoulême to Arbaud-Joucques, July 30, 1815. The heading on this letter: Gouvernement Général de S.A.R. Monseigneur le Duc d'Angoulême, Administration Générale.

[32] A.N., F⁷9657, Arbaud-Joucques to Minister, August 19, 1815.

[33] A.N., F⁷9049, "Réflexions sur l'écrit . . . ," n.d. [August 1815].

[34] Lauze de Peret, *Causes et précis,* pp. 159–160.

[35] C. Perrot, *Report on the Persecutions,* pp. 18–19.

[36] A.D. Gard, 6M22, J. Ducamp to prefect, August 31, 1821, reviews one such case, in renewing a demand for compensation.

The plundering, extortion, and destruction continued when these bands entered Nîmes. By the end of August responsible Protestant sources set the figure of damaged homes throughout the department at 300, of which 90 were country houses belonging to Protestants in Nîmes.[37] An official list of property destruction, admittedly incomplete, lists only six non-Protestant victims. Office-holders and *négociants* were the occupations most often affected.[38] Well-off Protestants were the favored prey:

There are not ten Protestants of some honest means in the city who have not been afflicted with some arbitrary contribution, and some losses through theft, which would have been punished by the galleys in former times.[39]

While only 100 registered complaints with the police that they had been victims of extortion, a Protestant source set at 2,000 the number of his co-religionists who had been subject to forced payments.[40]

It was risky for Protestants to walk through the city streets during this period. The Catholic lower classes, including the women among them, were considered dangerous. As described by one witness:

It was certainly rare that a Protestant dared to show himself in public. I saw some insulted while out walking; they were chased on Sundays, especially, at which time they were at the mercy of the *bas peuple*. This class forms at least four fifths of

---

[37] Arch. Cons. Nîmes, B53[24], president to Manuel Saumane, December 30, 1815. The same figures were restated in C. Perrot, *Report on the Persecutions*, p. 8.

[38] A.N., F[7]9049, Etat nominatif des personnes dont les propriétés ont été pillées, dévastées . . . , September [?], 1815.

[39] C. Durand, *Marseille, Nismes et ses environs*, p. 61.

[40] Marquis [Joseph-Charles-André] d'Arbaud-Joucques, *Troubles et agitations du Gard* . . . (Paris and Nîmes, 1818), pp. 70–71, in a point by point refutation, denies Perrot's figure of 2000 ransomings with the statement that only 100 complaints were registered with the police.

the population in Nîmes, and the kind of assurance shown by it was much less proud than arrogant or brutal.[41]

Protestant women were singled out for a strange beating. Skirts were lifted and the women paddled with a board whose protruding spikes formed a fleur-de-lys. Up to 40 women were victims of this scourging, and at least two died.[42]

The royalist bands in Nîmes joined freely those carrying out citizen's justice in bringing suspects to the jails. The police commissioner reported on July 25:

A great number of arrests have been made by the people *(le peuple)*, armed forces, and the civil and military authorities. [These were made] without warrants and most of the suspects have been put in prison without being inscribed in the prison register.[43]

The Ministry in Paris disapproved of the police commissioner's permissive attitude toward the arrests but was unable to suspend Angoulême's appointee, Vidal, from his post.[44]

To judge the suspects a military tribunal was set up composed of five to six Catholic royalists. The persons tried were those considered disloyal to the King during the Hundred Days. Members of the national guard of the Hundred Days, those who had joined the *fédérations,* and inactive soldiers on half-pay who had been unwilling to fight with the Duke in April were prime suspects.[45]

[41] Lauze de Peret, *Causes et précis*, p. 398.
[42] C. Perrot, *Report on the Persecutions*, pp. 18, 27, asserted that 30 to 40 women had been beaten in this way, and that eight or nine had died as a result. Arbaud-Joucques, *Troubles et agitations*, pp. 70–71, contended that only three or four women had been so beaten and that none had died.
[43] A.N., F⁷9049, Vidal to Minister, July 25, 1815.
[44] Vidal's functions were suspended in a letter of August 3, but Arbaud-Joucques found Vidal's presence necessary and demanded that his position as police commissioner be made official. A long correspondence on the subject exists in A.N., F⁷9049.
[45] A.N., F⁷9049, report signed "Vérité" to Minister, July 29, 1815.

Angoulême's appointees had passively accepted the denial of civil guarantees to Protestants during the early days of the liberation. They did so with the knowledge that during the Empire, the First Restoration and the Hundred Days, Protestants had controlled the municipal government and national guard and had been well represented in the lower courts. A terror directed against the Protestants would make it easier to purge these bodies and shift control of them to Catholic and royalist hands. Angoulême's representatives also hoped, in denying Protestants guarantees of personal security and property, to gain the support of the Catholic lower classes of the city, whose animosity was fed by envy of the rich and a tradition of religious intolerance.

The royalist authorities loyal to Angoulême did little to halt the depredations of the royalist bands through July and most of August. The special delegate, Bernis, in a proclamation in July, had implicitly condoned those acts as "certain unavoidable excesses of a great revolution."[46] By condoning the activities of royalist bands for more than a month, the appointees of Angoulême became tacit accomplices in their crimes. The number of civilians assassinated by royalist bands in July and August 1815 reached the figure of 100. Most were Protestants from Nîmes.[47]

Throughout the department the courts did not function during July, August, and early September. In Nîmes judges from both the appeal and district courts had withdrawn from public life, proscribed by royalists. Vidal reported their absence without sympathy:

The *Procureur-Général* of the royal court, M. Cavalier, the

[46] *Ibid.*

[47] C. Perrot, *Report on the Persecutions,* p. 18, set the figure in the department as high as 300, of which 200 were from Nîmes. These were the figures compiled by the president of the Protestant Consistory: See Arch. Cons. Nîmes, B53[24]. Ross, F.O. 27/130, report of January 21, 1816, estimated that there had been 200 killed in Nîmes, but this doubtless included those killed as members of the national guard protecting the garrison during the first day of the liberation. Arbaud-Joucques, *Troubles et agitations,* pp. 70–71, stated that no more than 70 persons had been killed in the entire department.

*Procureur du Roi,* M. Delpuch, and the substitute *Procureur du Roi,* Vincent St. Laurent, *fils,* have all been proscribed by the royalists. The first is in hiding, the second seldom shows himself, and the third is in flight. The second substitute has been absent the last three or four months: Mssrs. Bordariez, vice-president, and the respected judges of the court of first instance left Nîmes on July 15, and withdrew with the *fédérés* . . . all are pointed out as partisans of Napoleon and most as *fédérés.*[48]

Vidal wished to see these judges replaced, and not recalled to office.[49]

Vidal's prime concern in matters of justice was that the guilty parties of the Hundred Days be punished. In the absence of court magistrates the police commissioner took an active role in the interrogation of suspects. Rarely were men brought in simply for pillaging. When two men were arrested for trying to extort money from a local resident, Vidal justified the arrest not by their attempt to extort funds but by their past failure to campaign with Angoulême. He wrote to the Minister: "They are strongly suspected of Napoleonism . . . Neither one has campaigned with the Duke of Angoulême." [50] When Cavalier returned to his post as *procureur-général* in early September, he wrote to Vidal to announce that he did so reluctantly.[51] The police commissioner replied that his first concern as magistrate should be the punishment of those responsible for the massacre of Angoulême's troops at Arpaillargues in April.[52]

The threat to Protestant life and property in Nîmes from the incoming royalist bands, abetted by the royalist authorities, forced hundreds of Protestants to leave the city. A threat by Vidal

[48] A.N., F⁷9049, Vidal to Minister, August 22, 1815.
[49] A.N., F⁷9049, Vidal to Minister, August 28, 1815. A copy was sent to the Minister of Justice, September 9, 1815.
[50] A.N., F⁷9049, Vidal to Minister, August 15, 1815.
[51] A.N., F⁷9049, procureur-général to Vidal, September 7, 1815.
[52] A.N., F⁷9049, Vidal to procureur-général, September 11, 1815. See above, p. 46.

to confiscate the property of those who did not return by July 28 failed to stem the exodus.[53] The Cévenol villages, Lyons, and in some cases England and Switzerland received the refugees. A reliable source estimated that between July and October, 1815, 2,500 men had left the city—400 employers, 1,500 formerly employed workers, and 600 agricultural workers and artisans. With the men went as much as one and a half million francs in capital.[54] The contemporary account of an English visitor confirmed the disastrous effect of the flight of men and capital on the city's commerce and industry: "The largest manufactories are shut up; the proprietors have fled; and the silk trade, so prosperous in that city under the late government, is entirely ruined." [55]

The commercial and industrial crisis created by the emigration coincided with an agricultural crisis. Vidal, who rarely described economic and social conditions in his reports, took note of the dangers of a grain shortage, and a prolonged dry spell:

It is incumbent on me to inform Your Excellence of a very unfortunate circumstance which, because of its consequences, concerns the *Haute Police*. The grain harvest has been very bad, and I am not afraid to state that there is only enough grain in the Gard to feed her inhabitants for five or six months at the most. This fact has raised the price of first quality [grain] in a fifteen-day period from 50 to 67 francs for . . . ten decaliters and rye from 34 to 42 francs for the same measure.

It is therefore extremely urgent that the government take measures to insure the Gard adequate provisions and to lower the price of grain.

This measure is all the more pressing since the workshops have not yet resumed their activity and most of the workers are unemployed. In addition, because of the extreme drought that has

[53] A.N., F⁷9049, Vidal to Minister, July 25, 1815; C. Durand, *Marseille, Nismes et ses environs*, p. 55.
[54] A.N., F⁷9049, Eymard to Minister, November 29, 1815.
[55] C. Perrot, *Report on the Persecutions*, p. 19.

afflicted us for almost a month, the inhabitants of the countryside, most still armed, cannot work the land.[56]

Disarmament of the population, imperative in these circumstances, was extremely difficult. No serious effort was made to disarm the royalist bands until Austrian occupying troops entered the department in late August. Before that, from July 17 until August 25, only the homes of Bonapartist suspects had been searched for weapons and ammunition while members of the irregular royalist bands were allowed to retain their arms. Owing to difficulties in providing for Austrian troops in Provence, the royalist officials there had arranged for 6,000 to 8,000 troops to move into the Gard.[57] When the first contingent arrived in Nîmes on August 22,[58] it was used by the prefect Arbaud-Joucques to curtail for the first time the activities of royalist bands.

Obliged by the presence of the Austrian troops to leave Nîmes a band of 50 royalist irregulars marched up into the Cévennes. At Ners, 18 miles northwest of Nîmes, they were almost ambushed by fearful armed Protestant peasants grouped on the heights above them. This was the eve of the anniversary of the St. Bartholomew's Day massacre and the peasants were expecting violence. To quell the Cévenol Protestants the royalist band called in a unit of 800 Austrian troops, and in the encounter that followed 50 to 60 peasants were killed. As a punishment to the peasants those Austrian troops in the department who were not lodged in Nîmes were thereafter billeted in the Protestant communes.[59]

[56] A.N., F⁷9049, Vidal to Minister, August 19, 1815.

[57] A.N., F⁷9657, Austrian Intendant to Arbaud-Joucques, August 18, 1815; Arbaud-Joucques to Austrian Commandant, August 20, 1815 (copy).

[58] A.N., F⁷9049, proclamation of Arbaud-Joucques, August 23, 1815; joint proclamation with Austrian military officials, August 30, 1815.

[59] A.N., F⁷9049, Vidal to Minister, August 26, 1815; A.N., F⁷9049, Eymard to Minister of Police, November 29, 1815. See D. Robert, *Les Eglises Réformées*, p. 281 (footnote 1), for Cévenol expectations on the anniversary of St. Bartholomew's Day.

The disarmament operation in the department had yielded a large number of weapons of all sorts by September 1815[60] but was not an unqualified success. According to the commander of the department, over 10,000 rifles were collected along with 872 pistols, 817 bayonets, 1,486 sabers and swords, and 256 muskets. The bulk of this collection was distributed to the authorized national guard units in the department. However, despite the fact that Uzès had yielded up 2,000 weapons, and Vigan and Alais each twice that number, the Protestant communes to the north and northwest of Nîmes had not been substantially disarmed.[61] Furthermore the collection of weapons had been subject to scandalous abuses. An inspector reported later that numerous complaints had been made about the collection procedure:

Several mayors have told me that they wished to complain to you that guns were demanded of the people of their communes when they did not have any to surrender. The truth is that many residents of the communes of Gallargues and Aiguesvives have been obliged to buy some at Lunel, Aimargues and elsewhere. Members of the national guards were the ones who sold them guns so that they might themselves go out later [with the money] and buy rifles of better caliber.[62]

Despite the existence of an armed Protestant peasantry in the nearby Cévenol communes, a restrained calm had returned to Nîmes by early September.[63] This was broken in November by violence which showed the still insecure position of the Protestant community in the city. In a visit to Nîmes in early November Angoulême had promised members of the Consistory that on Sunday, November 12, they would be able to resume their re-

---

[60] A.D. Gard, 6M22, report of Maréchal de Camp Lagarde, September, 1815.
[61] A.N., F⁷9049, Eymard to Minister, November 20, 1815.
[62] A.D. Gard, 6M22, commissaire délégué in the Vaunage to Minister, January 11, 1816.
[63] A.N., F⁷9657, Arbaud-Joucques to Minister of Interior, September 5, 1815. A copy was sent to the Minister of Police.

ligious services, suspended since the liberation.[64] They were to be held where they had been since 1802, in the former chapel of the Ursuline convent.[65] General Lagarde, then commander of the army in the department, was made responsible for the safe conduct of the services.

For the occasion General Lagarde mustered a section of the national guard. It had been over two months since there had been major violence in the streets of Nîmes; when the church had filled up Lagarde assumed that he might leave the scene. During his absence a crowd of the Catholic lower classes began to pound at the doors. The din grew, striking fear among those confined within. Suddenly the doors burst apart and a mob poured in. Lagarde returned in time to discipline the national guard and to force back the crowd. Those who had sat through the services had vivid and frightening memories.[66]

Although the Protestants regained their homes successfully, Lagarde himself was wounded by a shot fired at him by one of the members of the national guard. There was little difficulty in identifying the would-be assassin,[67] but there were great problems in bringing him to trial. The culprit, Buisson, was a sergeant in the national guard company commanded by the son of

[64] Arch. Cons. Nîmes, B53[14], President of Consistory to Angoulême, n.d. [November 13, 1815]; Archives Privées, Papiers Vaublanc, Angoulême to Vaublanc, November 30, 1815.

[65] See above, footnote 7. These churches were sought by the Catholics, but the Protestant consistories did not want to establish a precedent by giving up their right to hold services in them. See letter to Daniel Encontre, professor at the Protestant theological seminary of Montauban, September 4, 1815, in D. Bourchenin, "La Terreur Blanche à Montauban et Nîmes (1815) d'après quelques lettres inédites," *Bulletin de la Société de l'histoire du Protestantisme français* LIX (Paris, 1910), 516. Archives Privées, Papiers Vaublanc, Angoulême to Vaublanc, November 30, 1815; A.N., F[7]9049, Report of mayor of Nîmes, December 19, 1815.

[66] Arch. Cons. Nîmes, B53[14], copy of letter from president of consistory to Angoulême, November 13, 1815; A.N., F[7]9049, letter from Rose Rochefort and other unsigned letters to Minister, week of November 12, 1815.

[67] A.D. Gard, 6M22, unsigned letter to Lagarde, dated November 12, 1815; A.N., F[7]9049, Arbaud-Joucques to Minister, November 13, 1815.

police commissioner Vidal. Buisson had been seen entering Vidal's house the morning of the crime.[68] No arrests were made that day or in the days that followed. The propertyless element in the national guard was held to be responsible for the disorder and a reorganization of the guard took place in which the property qualification was reintroduced.[69] The suspect left the department and almost a year elapsed before he was brought back in custody to Nîmes.[70]

When Buisson was put on trial in the *cour d'assises* of Nîmes in February 1817, the government expected an indictment. The jury of twelve had been hand-picked and consisted largely of office-holders living outside Nîmes.[71] It was expected to be responsive to the government's wishes. However, in handling the specific charges made against the accused, the jury did not carry out its duties properly. Buisson was found guilty of carrying a concealed weapon but no recommendation was made for punishment on that count. Though it was found that the accused had attacked General Lagarde, the jury accepted the argument of the defense that he had been provoked without legitimate motive.[72] A decree of February 9, 1817 acquitted the suspect. The royalist secret organization, the *Société de Balse,* had done everything in its power to gain that acquittal.[73]

The general public in England had been made aware of the character of the political reaction in the Cévennes area by the

[68] A.N., F⁷9049, Garde des Sceaux to Minister of Police (personal), December 21, 1815.

[69] A.N., F⁷9049, Arrêté de la Préfecture concernant la Réorganization de la Garde Nationale de Nismes, November 17, 1815; Arbaud-Joucques to Minister, November 20, 1815.

[70] A.N., F⁷9049, Arbaud-Joucques to Minister, September 20, 1816.

[71] A.N., F⁷9049, prefect to Minister, January 31, 1817; prefect to Minister, February 9, 1817; Minister to prefect, February 19, 1817.

[72] A.N., F⁷9049, commissaire général de police to Minister, February 9, 1817.

[73] A.N., F⁷9049, Observation sur le procès. . . , n.d. [February, 1817]; Lauze de Peret, *Causes et précis,* p. 392.

descriptions of English travelers.[74] These pointed up the destruction of Protestant temples in Bas Languedoc and the mistreatment and subsequent emigration of Protestants from Nîmes. The information had been gathered by members of the nonestablished religious bodies in England, who shared with the French Calvinists a minority position in the political and religious life of their country. On the occasion of the White Terror in the Gard they expressed sympathy and support.

This sympathy took institutional form when two separate bodies of English Protestants, one an association of Dissenters, the other a society for freedom of conscience, which included some Anglican members, met separately on November 21, 1815.[75] For these bodies the reaction in the Gard was a simple matter of religious persecution, which demanded a show of solidarity. A circular letter of November 28, 1815 made their position clear:

We have ascertained with a precision too accurate for our wishes and hopes that for a long period our Protestant brethren have been exposed to merciless persecution by the agents of a despotic and cruel fanaticism. With such facts before us, as Protestant Dissenters, and the descendants of men who achieved the liberties of Britain and diffused through Europe the most enlightened principles, we could not mistake in deciding it was our duty to give a distinct and public expression of our sentiments.[76]

To express their views the two groups sent circular letters to the French pastors, collected funds, and tried to have their gov-

[74] Helen-Marie Williams, daughter of a Methodist minister, and Clement Perrot, a Presbyterian minister from Jersey, both made trips at this time and published reports.

[75] Arch. Cons. Nîmes, B53[27], circular of November 28, 1815 indicates date of the Dissenters' meeting; Alice Wemyss, "L'Angleterre et la Terreur blanche de 1815 dans le Midi," *Annales du Midi,* LXXIII (1961), 293, comments on these groups.

[76] Arch. Cons. Nîmes, B53[27], circular letter of November 28, 1815.

ernment issue, through diplomatic channels, a protest against the abuse of Protestants in France.[77] Wellington assured them that such a protest would be made.[78] The English government eventually sent its own representative to investigate the position of Protestants in the Midi.[79]

In France the interpretation of events in the Gard had become an issue in the war between the constitutional moderates and the Ultras. Ardent royalists in Angoulême's camp preferred to see attacks on Protestants in the Gard as simply political retribution; constitutional moderates in France and Protestants in both France and England were more prone to see simply a violation of the religious guarantees of the Charter.

Among those upholding the position of the constitutional moderates was the liberal writer of Protestant family, Benjamin Constant. He argued, quite naively, that Protestants in the Gard had never been influential politically under the Empire.[80] Furthermore, given the guarantees of the Charter, no attack on them could be justified. He was quite right about the guarantees of the Charter excluding a persecution of Protestants, but obedience to

[77] Arch. Cons. Nîmes, B53[27], circular letter of December 10, 1815. The Protestant ministers of the Gard, Haute-Garonne, Tarn-et-Garonne, and Gers quickly notified their prefects, when they received the circular letters: See Archives Privées, Papiers Vaublanc, Angoulême to Vaublanc, January 2, 1816; A.N., F[7]9049, Arbaud-Joucques to Minister, January 3, 1816.

[78] Arch. Cons. Nîmes, B53[27], circular letter of November 28, 1815. Wellington did make a veiled protest the following February, when events in the Midi were no longer a major issue. See Arthur Wellesley, Duke of Wellington, *Supplementary Despatches, Correspondence, and Memoranda* (London, 1863), XI, 309–310, for a letter of concern to Louis XVIII, dated February 29, 1816. The Midi was not mentioned.

[79] See reports of Ross, F.O. 27. The return of Colonel Ross to England on January 28, 1816, is mentioned in Wellington, *Supplementary Despatches*, XI, 295, letter to Castlereagh, January 29, 1816.

[80] Benjamin Constant, *Lettres à M. Charles Durand, avocat, en réponse aux questions contenues dans . . . Marseille, Nismes et ses environs en 1815* (Paris, 1818). Lewis Gwynn, "La Terreur blanche et l'application de la loi Decazes dans le département du Gard (1815–17)," *Annales Historiques de la Révolution Française* (Paris, April–June 1964), 174–193, presents a similar thesis of unwarranted religious persecution in an article enlivened by some new material on earlier royalist activity in the Gard.

the law presupposed a widespread public support for its guarantees or, at the least, public authority committed to the defense of equal rights for Protestants. Neither condition existed in the Gard at the beginning of the Second Restoration.

Those who held that this was a politically inspired reaction were quite correct. Political goals in the South had been clearly formulated by the Ultra leadership: ". . . the punishment of all the traitors and the occupancy of all offices by pure and proven royalists is indispensable." [81] The victims of this policy in the Gard were mainly Protestants. However, when René de Bernis and the prefect Arbaud-Joucques argued that a political reaction was not persecution, they avoided discussion of the role that persecution of Protestants had played in forcing political changes.[82] In fact, popular anti-Protestant feelings had been made to serve the cause of radical royalist politics in the department.

In November 1815 the dialogue over the reaction in the Gard was carried to the floor of the Chamber of Deputies. By then a Chamber dominated by Ultras was occupied with the passage of repressive legislation. It had little patience with liberals or constitutional moderates. When a call to examine the events in the Gard was made from the floor, it was quickly drowned by cries of protest. At that juncture the majority of the Chamber did not wish to bring into question the abuses of a local reaction. Their major interest was to extend the political reaction initiated in the South. In so doing they hoped to root out what they considered to be subversive elements in French public life and establish a moral and political climate friendly to their cause.

[81] A.N., F⁷9049, royalist petition to King, reprinted in *Journal Officiel du Gard,* August 12, 1815.
[82] R. de Bernis, *Précis,* pp. 57 ff.; J.-C.-A. Arbaud-Joucques, *Troubles et agitations,* pp. 70 ff.

# IV

# REPRESSIVE LEGISLATION

The elections of August 1815 brought to Paris a strongly royalist and politically inexperienced assembly. Of the deputies, scarcely one man in six had sat in any of the preceding assemblies.[1] The aristocracy of the Old Regime was represented on just a little less than half the benches. Seventy-three of these 176 nobles had been émigrés. It was this assembly that Louis XVIII qualified as "introuvable." Inexperienced as legislators, the members of the Chamber nevertheless united effectively on almost every piece of repressive legislation that came before them. An important factor in explaining their cohesiveness was the frequency with which they consulted one another about political matters.

The new deputies gathered almost nightly in the first few months of the Chamber's life in meetings which were in character a cross between the salon and the political caucus. The number of separate royalist groups meeting in this fashion expressed the variety of viewpoints in the royalist camp. Villèle described them to his father in a letter written shortly after the new session opened:

---

[1] These figures are based on the composition of a Chamber of 381 deputies in January 1816. See G. de Bertier, *La Restauration* (Paris, 1955), p. 176. Jean Bécarud, "La noblesse dans les Chambres (1815–1830)," *Revue internationale d'histoire politique et constitutionnelle* (Paris, 1953), p. 192 and table p. 202, says that 54 percent of the deputies were nobles but that eight had been ennobled during the Empire. The process by which these deputies were elected needs to be studied department by department and has not yet been the subject of extensive research.

Almost every night I have to remain until eleven or midnight in meetings of deputies where matters to be submitted to the Chamber are discussed. This part of our preoccupations is the most curious. There exist perhaps ten or twelve groups of this sort, without counting that of M. Voyer d'Argenson, which is frequented exclusively by former representatives of the Chamber of Bonaparte and by other deputies with similar opinions. You understand that I do not got to that group but I am always invited to the others, which are all royalist in character. In some they revile the Ministers and they wish to get rid of the worst of them. In others conspiracies are seen as ready to break out everywhere and it is believed that France must have a civil war as the only means of salvation and regeneration. In another, it is thought that the Ministry and the King are doing all that they can and that they must be supported. Everywhere there are the best intentions in the world, but what a Tower of Babel; what confusion, not of languages, but of points of view . . .[2]

The Chevaliers de la Foi were a controlling force in the Chamber's majority. They successfully ensured that among the officers of the assembly and on all the committees their viewpoint would be represented.[3] This was achieved despite the fact that few of the commonly acknowledged leaders of the right could now be recognized with certainty as members of the Chevaliers. Bonald denied belonging to a Congrégation although his denial cannot be taken at face value. La Bourdonnaye was perhaps too much of a schemer to have been taken into the group. Vitrolles, hoping to be an emissary between royalist factions, had not joined. Among the leaders of the Chamber of Deputies, as opposed to the rank and file, Villèle's membership is the only one about which we can be sure.[4]

[2] Letter of October 18, 1815, quoted in Joseph de Villèle, *Mémoires et correspondance du Comte de Villèle* (Paris, 1888), I, 367.

[3] G. de Bertier, *Un type d'ultra-royaliste: le comte Ferdinand de Bertier et l'énigme de la Congrégation* (Paris, 1948), p. 187, citing F. de Bertier, "Souvenirs."

[4] G. de Bertier, *Le comte Ferdinand de Bertier* (Paris, 1948), pp. 188–190.

One meeting-place of the Chevaliers de la Foi was the Palais Bourbon itself, in the offices of the financial administrator of the Chamber of Deputies, the Marquis de Puyvert.[5] Their greatest influence, however, was felt in larger groups in which, as a hard core, they could press their views on others. One of the most celebrated of these large political salons was that held in the home of the Parisian deputy, Piet. By January 1816 it drew more than half the Chamber.[6] There, deputies from the provinces could learn about parliamentary procedure, discuss issues, and promote their own careers.

In caucuses like these deputies were able to work out a common strategy in dealing with the Ministry. Although they were divided on major questions of policy, there were certain areas in which royalist deputies could come to agreement. One of these was the need to maintain the prerogatives of the Chamber. Although the Charter had left legislative initiative to the King and his Ministers, it had provided certain ways in which the Chamber could assert its authority. The power to suggest legislation to the Ministry was perhaps the weakest of these. In the area of legislation, the Chamber expressed itself most effectively through the legislative committees to which every bill had to be referred. In the review of ministerial proposals in committee the government could be brought to accept modifications of text, or face the prospect of a bill being reported to the Chamber accompanied by a set of the committee's amendments for separate consideration. Through its legislative committees the Chamber regained some of the legislative initiative formally denied to it by the Charter of 1814.

Though an opposition between the Ministry and the Chamber

[5] See Puyvert, *Livre de raison,* quoted in G. de Bertier, *Le comte Ferdinand de Bertier,* p. 187 (footnote 20). See also Prosper Duvergier de Hauranne, *Histoire du gouvernement parlementaire en France* (Paris, 1859), III, 267.

[6] See Duvergier de Hauranne, *Histoire,* III, 293; G. de Bertier, *Le comte Ferdinand de Bertier,* pp. 187–188; Etienne-Denis de Pasquier, *Histoire de mon temps: Mémoires du Chancelier Pasquier* (Paris, 1894), IV, 12.

of Deputies could have been foreseen on purely constitutional grounds, this opposition was not sustained by simple questions of prerogative. The debates over repressive legislation provide an illustration of the substantive aspects of the conflict shaped by political differences. Royalists in the Chamber used their authority to amend legislation that seemed too mild to them and abstained from altering bills that pleased them. An analysis of the opposition between deputies and Ministers on the principal pieces of repressive legislation indicates the process by which the legal channels for the reaction were created.

The possibility of the trial or proscription of Bonapartists as traitors was raised shortly after the defeat of the French armies at Waterloo. Such a measure was considered urgent by those in Louis XVIII's entourage who attributed Napoleon's success the preceding March to a conspiracy made possible by the King's own leniency at the First Restoration. Two royal declarations on the subject of political responsibility for the Hundred Days had been made en route to Paris from Ghent. A declaration had first been issued from Cateau-Cambrésis, when Louis was under the influence of Dambray, an aging diehard who had been Minister of Justice under the First Restoration. It threatened in the broadest terms to punish those who had supported Napoleon during the Hundred Days. Royalists who were satisfied with this proclamation were to be disappointed with the modifying declaration which soon followed. At the next stage of his journey, when Louis had been joined by Talleyrand, a new statement was issued. At Cambrai, on June 28, 1815, the King advanced a more conciliatory formula:

I promise . . . to pardon, in the case of misled Frenchmen, all that has happened from the day I left Lille [March 23, 1815] amid so many tears to the day I re-entered Cambrai [June 28, 1815] amid so many acclamations.

However, the blood of my subjects has flowed through a treason of which the annals of the world offer no example . . . I must, therefore, for the dignity of my throne, exempt from the pardon the instigators and the authors of this horrible plot. They will be designated for the vengeance of the law by both Chambers, which I propose to assemble shortly.[7]

Pressure for the punishment of "instigators and authors" of the Hundred Days came from without the country as well as within. Of the Allies, the British were at first particularly insistent. Although the surrender agreement with the Allies signed at Saint-Cloud on July 3 had stipulated that a general amnesty would be proclaimed, and that all those who wished to emigrate for political reasons would be allowed to do so without loss of property, the British advised the French King neither to sign this treaty nor feel personally bound by those provisions.[8] Prominent British newspapers demanded the punishment of Bonapartists and *The Times* even suggested a list of the guilty.[9] Their insistence made it seem inadvisable for Louis XVIII to wait until the Chambers could be assembled and the Minister of Police, Joseph Fouché, was assigned the task of singling out in advance those who were responsible for Bonaparte's triumph.

However, the selection of Fouché for such a task could only mean that Louis XVIII had no stomach for a far-reaching purge of Bonapartists. Fouché had been a prominent cabinet minister

[7] The text of the latter was included in the proclamation, "Roy aux français," issued on July 16, 1815, Arch. Préf. Paris, A^419. See also *Archives Parlementaires de 1787 à 1860* (Paris, 1869), Deuxième série, XV, 2, for the text of both declarations.

[8] For a good discussion of the British attitude in the context of the agreement signed at Saint-Cloud, see Harold Kurtz, *The Trial of Marshal Ney, His Last Years and Death* (New York, 1957), pp. 199–205. For instances of Allied diplomatic pressure, see Pozzo di Borgo to Talleyrand, July 13, 1815, Archives des Affaires Etrangères, 691; and confidential report to Wellington, July 19, 1815, *Supplementary Despatches*, XI, 45: both are cited in Jean Thiry, *Les débuts de la Deuxième Restauration* (Paris, 1947), p. 260.

[9] Duvergier de Hauranne, *Histoire*, III, 214.

during the Hundred Days and had a political past that extended to the early days of the Revolution. The severe and unforgiving Duchess of Angoulême, daughter of Louis XVI, certainly would continue to consider him *persona non grata* at court. What interest could he have in condemning associates of the past? It was clear that even the most turncoat behaviour would not redeem him in the eyes of his enemies.

Fouché tried successfully to avoid making the final selection of victims his own personal responsibility. According to a knowledgeable colleague, Fouché finally presented such a lengthy and ill-chosen list of names to his fellow Ministers that those choices were discredited.[10] At the same time in *L'Indépendant,* a newspaper under his control, he waged a propaganda campaign to excuse those whom the Ultras could not forgive. He tried especially to exonerate the regicides of the Convention, and those who in March of 1815, before Louis XVIII's departure, had accepted service with Napoleon.[11] However, he did think that the publication of a definitive list of exemptions would be desirable. By limiting the number of those held responsible for the Hundred Days such a list might end the wave of arrests being carried out by royalist groups in the Midi.[12]

The so-called amnesty decree proclaimed on July 24, 1815 was in fact an indictment of 57 persons. It followed the declaration of Cambrai in considering as treasonous any support for Napoleon before March 23, the date of Louis' departure from France, and after July 8, the date of Louis' return to Paris. Two general cate-

[10] E.-D. de Pasquier, *Histoire de mon temps,* III, 368–369. However, Vitrolles, whom Fouché had befriended during the Hundred Days, defends his benefactor against this charge. See E. de Vitrolles, *Mémoires et relations politiques,* III, 146, where it is claimed that Fouché presented a list of only 60 names.

[11] *L'Indépendant,* July 14 and July 25, 1815, cited in L. Madelin, *Fouché,* 2 ed. rev. (Paris, 1903), II, 454. The editor of this newspaper was the liberal deputy, Manuel, a protégé of Fouché.

[12] Louis Madelin, *Fouché,* II, 454–455. The critical ministerial comment made on Vidal's report of arbitrary arrests in the Gard, A.N., $F^7$9049, July 25, 1815, sustained this view for it noted reprovingly that the forthcoming amnesty decree would indicate which persons could be arrested.

gories of guilt were established:[13] the first for those who had participated violently in the overthrow of royal authority and the second for those who had merely favored Bonaparte's return in public statements.

In the latter category were 38 civil and military figures and they were ordered to leave Paris within three days. Pending action by the legislature they were to be placed under surveillance in the interior. Some members of this group were proscribed for reasons that had more to do with political conduct during the Revolution than the Hundred Days. Included were some members of the Convention who had voted the death of Louis XVI and had compounded their crime in royalist eyes by supporting the regime of the Hundred Days. Others were men who had accepted a ministerial position from the Emperor soon after his arrival in Paris on March 20 and before Louis XVIII's departure from Lille on March 23. Thus the list included Fouché's colleagues of the Convention, men like Barère, Garnier de Saintes, and Lepelletier, and more recent collaborators like Savary and Maret. Old comrades like Carnot and Thibaudeau were also on this list.[14]

The first category was reserved exclusively for military men.

---

[13] Vitrolles, *Mémoires et relations politiques*, III, 146–147, claimed responsibility for the principle of two categories. Names in the two groups were as follows: (1) Ney, Labédoyère, les deux frères Lallemant, Drouet-d'Erlon, Lefebvre-Desnouettes, Ameilh, Brayer, Gilly, Mouton-Duvernet, Grouchy, Clausel, Laborde, Debelle, Bertrand, Drouot, Cambronne, Lavalette, Rovigo; (2) Soult, Alix, Excelmans, Bassano, Marbot, Felix Lepelletier, Boulay (de la Meurthe), Méhée, Fressinet, Thibaudeau, Carnot, Vandamne, Lamarque (général), Lobau, Harel, Piré, Barrère, Arnault, Pomereuil, Regnaud de Saint-Jean d'Angély, Arrighi de Padoue, Dejean fils, Garreau, Réal, Bouvier-Dumolard, Merlin (de Douai), Durbach, Dirat, Defermont, Bory-Saint-Vincent, Félix Desportes, Garnier de Saintes, Millinet, Hullin, Cluys, Courtin, Forbin-Janson fils aîné, La Lorgne-Dideville. The decree appeared in *Le Moniteur*, July 26, 1815. The text to be found in *Archives Parlementaires*, XV, 25, provided the basis for the above spelling.

[14] L. Madelin, *Fouché*, II, 455–456. References to the sources are given. See also Arch. Pref. Police, Paris, A^327, for the dossiers of individuals affected by the decree of July 24, 1815.

Nineteen high-ranking officers were to be sent before military tribunals for treason. Included in this group were those who, like Marshal Ney, had failed to maintain their oath of loyalty in March and others, like General Gilly, who had fought against royalist volunteers in the South. Some had simply refused to give their loyalty to Louis when news of his return to Paris on July 8 was announced. Fouché did his best to help these men flee France by providing passports and assistance.[15]

Of the 19 marshals and generals exempted from the amnesty Ney was the most illustrious. Louis XVIII had recognized that the capture of Marshal Ney in the Lot had ultimately proven a disservice to the royal cause.[16] Ney's military service to the Empire and his personal qualities had won him a great public following. He had been warned in advance by Fouché to leave the country. Nevertheless, certain that he could prove his innocence, Ney had insisted on being tried. After successfully contesting the jurisdiction of a military tribunal, he was allowed to appear before the Chamber of Peers, sitting in judgment on a Marshal of France. In the trial, Ney's lawyers defended him cleverly but not brilliantly.[17] The verdict was against him. On December 7, 1815, Ney was removed from his small second-floor room in the Luxemburg palace, and instead of being brought to the Champ de Mars, where the government feared a crowd would gather, was shot in the gardens of the Avenue de l'Observatoire.

Unfavorable public reaction to his execution presented the Ministry with an opportune moment for the introduction of a generous amnesty bill to supplement the King's decree. The British public no longer thirsted for the punishment of war crim-

---

[15] L. Madelin, *Fouché*, II; Duvergier de Hauranne, *Histoire*, III, 215–219.

[16] See Louis' statement, quoted in G. de Bertier, *La Restauration* (Paris, 1955), 180.

[17] The record of the trial may be found in *Archives Parlementaires*, XV, in the debates of the Chamber of Peers on November 11, 16, 17, and 23; and December 4, 5, and 6. For a recent and appreciative study of Ney and his trial, see Harold Kurtz, *The Trial of Marshal Ney, His Last Years and Death* (New York, 1957).

inals, and public opinion in France and England had been alerted to the excesses of the reaction in the South by pamphlets and newspaper reports. A more extensive amnesty proposal was presented to the Chamber for consideration by Armand-Emmanuel de Richelieu, the Minister closest to the King, a few hours after the execution of Marshal Ney.

Richelieu's bill was designed to end doubts about further sanctions against those involved in the Hundred Days, and to give the Chamber an opportunity to decide the punishment of the thirty-odd individuals then under surveillance as a result of the King's earlier decree. The bill read on December 7 pardoned all who had taken part, directly or indirectly, in the Hundred Days, except those named in the decree of July 24, the Bonaparte family, and those against whom court proceedings had already been instituted before the law went into effect.[18] The terms of this measure, exempting from prosecution for political reasons all but a tiny fraction of those associated with the regime of the Hundred Days, did not please the ultra-royalist Chamber of Deputies.

The Chamber had on its own initiative, before Richelieu introduced the Ministry's bill, made plans to suggest to the King more punitive action against Bonapartist traitors. In early November, when Ney was being tried by the Chamber of Peers, a committee of the Chamber of Deputies was meeting in secret to work out a proposal. This legislative committee had been sifting over suggestions made by various deputies. The most elaborate of these, and the most important for the course of later debate, was a proposal by François de la Bourdonnaye for the specification of five classes of criminals, all to be exempted from an amnesty.[19] First were those who had corresponded with the Emperor at Elba to facilitate his return; second, those who had, before

---

[18] See *Archives Parlementaires*, XV, 422–423. Richelieu proposed that the 38 persons on the second list be excluded from France within two months.

[19] *Ibid.*, pp. 215–244. This proposal was made on November 12. The secret committee to consider amnesty proposals was named on November 13: see *ibid.*, pp. 231–234.

March 23, accepted ministerial posts from the Emperor; third, those prefects who had recognized Napoleon before March 23; fourth, military men commanding divisions or parts thereof who had recognized the Emperor before he entered Paris; fifth, those generals who had led their troops against royalist armies during the Hundred Days. Individuals in most of these categories had been included in the first list of 57 on July 24, but that list had not pretended to include all those responsible for each crime specified by La Bourdonnaye. Such broad exclusions from an amnesty were absolutely unacceptable to Richelieu and his Ministers. They appeared justified only if one accepted the Ultras' assumption that the Hundred Days was the result of a premeditated and far-flung conspiracy within France.

Following the usual practice, Richelieu's bill, after its first reading on the floor of the Chamber, was referred to a legislative committee for consideration. The committee of nine to which it was sent included five men who had sat previously on the Chamber's secret committee, the one to which La Bourdonnaye had submitted his proposals. These five were Villèle, Bertier de Sauvigny, Chifflet, Corbière, and Pardessus. They were joined by Germiny, Duvergier de Hauranne, Cotton, and Cardonnel. In a six to three vote, this committee reported Richelieu's proposal with a set of amendments that supported La Bourdonnaye's list of exclusions.[20]

Richelieu had tried, unsuccessfully, to influence the committee in at least two ways during its deliberations. Turning first to persuasion, he invited Villèle and the other members of the committee to dinner. Invited at the same time were one or two fellow Ministers, and a few members of the Chamber known to be favorable to the government's position. The King's wishes were explained at length.[21] A second means of influencing the com-

---

[20] See Villèle, *Mémoires,* I, 410–411; Duvergier de Hauranne, *Histoire,* III, 313. Duvergier de Hauranne's father, along with Germiny and Cotton, formed the dissenting minority.

[21] See letter of Villèle to father, December 17, 1815, in Villèle, *Mémoires,* I, 412.

mittee's deliberations lay in the Ministry's control over high public offices sought by members of the Chamber. The Ministry could always bring pressure to bear on a deputy by blocking or furthering his quest for advancement. Thus, Corbière, the *rapporteur* for the committee, found a judicial appointment barred to him because he supported La Bourdonnaye's exemptions from the amnesty. He was denied a position as *procureur-général* at the royal court of Rennes, a post for which he had already been nominated.[22]

In addition to supporting the exclusion from an amnesty of the five groups described earlier, the legislative committee wished to exempt directly from the amnesty those regicides of the Convention who had openly supported Napoleon. Of the more than 400 members of the Convention who had voted in some way for the death of Louis XVI, those who had "relapsed" during the Hundred Days, by either supporting Napoleon's Additional Act or accepting public office, were to be affected. They were to be deprived of their civil rights, including the right to own property, and were to be expelled from the territory of France. Furthermore, those whose guilt had been determined by the proper bodies were to be made responsible through levies for the cost of the Hundred Days.[23]

The discussion of these proposals provided the most exciting and controversial moments in the parliamentary session of 1815–16. Fifty-four persons enrolled with the secretaries to speak for or against the government's measure.[24] When the Chamber proceeded to a vote on January 6 each article of the government's measure was considered separately.[25] Despite the controversy

---

[22] See Villèle to father, December 26, 1815, and January 7, 1816, in Villèle, *Mémoires*, I, 425–444.

[23] *Archives Parlementaires*, XV, 613–618. The six articles of Richelieu's bill were presented along with four proposed amendments.

[24] Achille de Vaulabelle, *Histoire des Deux Restaurations jusqu'à la chute de Charles X*, 2nd ed. (Paris, 1847), IV, 34. The bill and the proposed amendments were discussed January 2, 3, 4, 5, and 6. See proceedings for those days in *Archives Parlementaires*, XV.

[25] Voting began on January 6. See *Archives Parlementaires*, XV, 712 ff. especially.

there was broad agreement on the first two articles, which merely confirmed those exemptions made by the King himself in his amnesty decree of July 24. By royal compromise an agreement was also worked out on the exile of Napoleon Bonaparte's family, stating more strongly the exclusion of his family and descendants, to the degree of uncle and nephew, in perpetuity.

The assembly was more divided, however, on the crucial question of further limiting the amnesty by accepting the amendments of the legislative committee. The government had refused to incorporate these exceptions into its amnesty bill and they had to be voted on separately as amendments. While argument was running in favor of the amendments, the moderate Duvergier de Hauranne, in a parliamentarian's gambit, moved to consider the preceding question. In so doing, he was moving to end debate on the amendments and to vote on the government's position.[26] Many provincial nobles, inexperienced in parliamentary tactics, appear to have been confused by the procedure and left unsure about which question was being moved.[27] When those taking the affirmative position rose to express their vote, it was not clear where the majority lay. The assembly then proceeded to a secret vote. La Bourdonnaye's exceptions were rejected but by a margin of only nine votes. Had they been voted, and the legislation accepted by the King and the Chamber of Peers, at least 850 persons would have been condemned to deportation or death.[28]

There remained the fate of the regicides of the Convention who had aided Napoleon or who had received favors from him. Despite the opposition of Richelieu, who argued the need to respect the King's implicit reconciliation with the regicides, expressed in the Charter,[29] the Chamber would not be won over.

[26] See Duvergier de Hauranne, *Histoire,* p. 329. He was justly proud of his father's defense of a minority position.

[27] A. de Vaulabelle, *Histoire des Deux Restaurations,* IV, 43 (footnote 1).

[28] The Minister of Police presented to the King a list of 850 persons who would be affected by these exceptions: *Ibid.,* p. 35 (footnote 1).

[29] See Article 11 of the Charter of 1814, quoted above, p. 1.

When Richelieu stressed the importance of preserving a royal prerogative to grant amnesty, used with such excellent results by Henri IV in 1594, Corbière improved upon the Minister's history by pointing out the proscription decrees which had preceded that amnesty.[30] De Béthisy spoke for the ultra-royalists in the Chamber in distinguishing between the right of amnesty and the right to pardon convicted persons. The King, of course, was to be allowed to maintain the latter.[31] The article exempting the relapsed regicides from the amnesty was passed 334–22.

The King, who was not prepared either to dissolve his Chamber or to dismiss his Ministers, decided to accept the bill as amended by the Chamber. In its amended form, the bill marked a retreat from the Ministers' original position. Many more than the original 57 would now be exempted from the amnesty. Nevertheless, it would be difficult to identify those regicides of the Convention who had supported Napoleon during the Hundred Days,[32] and the 850 additional exemptions desired by La Bourdonnaye had been rejected in a close and confused vote by the legislature. The bill was presented to the Chamber of Peers for a vote on January 9, 1816. It was passed 120 to 21 and on January 12 became law.

Some ultra-royalists, however, felt cheated by the guarantees of the amnesty law. They looked for a loophole in the law by which they could bring more of Napoleon's supporters to trial. Relying on the clause which stated that all those against whom proceedings had begun in courts of justice would be exempt from the conditions of the amnesty, they prevailed on the Duke of Feltre,

[30] *Archives Parlementaires*, XV, 614. Stanley Mellon, *The Political Uses of History: A Study of Historians in the French Restoration* (Stanford, 1958), offers excellent insight into the place of historical argument in political debates during the Restoration.

[31] *Ibid.*, pp. 717–718. Clément Trinquelaque, a deputy from the Gard, proposed that the amnesty include royalists charged with crimes against individuals in the Midi and the West, "men who in their zeal for the royalist cause may have gone astray." It was rejected on constitutional grounds: *Ibid.*, pp. 713–714.

[32] See A.N., F1e153–169 (carton 3) for evidence of the difficulty the police had in deciding who were truly regicides and who had relapsed.

as Minister of War, to expedite proceedings against some of Napoleon's generals. The charge was to be treason, an offense punishable by death under article 57 of the penal code. Feltre is reported to have used the telegraph to have certain proceedings initiated before the law went into effect.[33]

One of those affected by this intervention was General Travot.[34] Travot, whose name was not among the 57 excluded from the King's amnesty on July 24, would have been affected by La Bourdonnaye's additions. He was one of the Napoleonic generals who had led their men against royalist groupings during the Hundred Days. Travot had been sent in this period to the Vendée to use his authority in containing the royalists. He had carried out this task with recognized moderation. At the head of the military tribunal judging him for treason was General Canuel who, ironically, had once led the Republican armies into the Vendée under the Convention. The death penalty was voted but Louis XVIII commuted it to 20 years of imprisonment.

Similarly affected were two other generals, Chartran and Mouton-Duvernet.[35] The first, like Travot, had not been excluded from the King's amnesty decree. Chartran had volunteered his services to Angoulême in March but had later gone over to the Emperor. He was responsible for the tricolor's being raised in Toulouse during the Hundred Days. His sentence to death by a military tribunal was not commuted. In the case of Mouton-Duvernet, Feltre's intervention merely expedited trial by a military tribunal. He had already been excluded from the King's amnesty. Mouton-Duvernet, made commander of Valence by Louis XVIII, had been one of the first generals to go over to Napoleon. From Lyons he had organized the army which marched against the Duke of Angoulême. He, too, was con-

---

[33] Duvergier de Hauranne, *Histoire*, III, 334.

[34] *Ibid.*, pp. 334–335; E.-D. de Pasquier, *Histoire de mon temps*, IV, 66. Pasquier was a close friend of Travot.

[35] See E.-D. de Pasquier, *Histoire de mon temps*, IV, 66–67.

demned by a military tribunal, and in July of 1816 was shot. Lesser military figures were also indicted before the bill became law but few were punished by death.[36]

The protection offered to citizens against abuses of police power was quite limited under French law. The Charter of 1814 had recognized only the rights of conscience and property as inviolable. Liberties of social significance, such as those of assembly and association, were not mentioned. Freedom from arbitrary arrest, like freedom of the press, was recognized subject to subsequent limitation by legislation: "No one may be arrested or prosecuted except in cases envisaged by the law, and according to the form which the law prescribes."[37] The law, expressed in relevant articles of the penal code, had specified that individuals could be detained for a maximum of only three days before being brought into court. However, detention without provision for trial had been allowed for one year without review by administrative order, in cases affecting the security of the state. The latter provision had been introduced by imperial decree in 1810.[38]

By extending the authority of the police to detain suspects without trial, ultra-royalists in the Chamber of Deputies hoped to continue their war on Napoleon's supporters. A bill to this effect was introduced in the Chamber by Elie Decazes, Fouché's successor as Minister of Police, in the second week of the session of 1815–16.[39] Under the proposed law, any person, civilian or mili-

---

[36] See, for example, Archives de la Guerre, C¹⁸73, Events of April 3, 1815, for the prosecution of lesser military figures for establishing Bonaparte's government in Nîmes on April 3. Proceedings were authorized because they had begun before the amnesty bill became law on January 12, 1816.

[37] Article 4 of the Charter of 1814.

[38] See Paul Bastid, *Les institutions politiques de la monarchie parlementaire française (1814–1848)* (Paris, 1954), pp. 359–363; Jacques Godechot, *Les institutions de la France sous la Révolution et l'Empire* (Paris, 1951), pp. 542–543.

[39] Presented on October 18, 1815: see *Archives Parlementaires*, XV, 78–80. Fouché had been forced out as Minister of Police on September 15, 1815: see L. Madelin, *Fouché*, II, 483–486.

tary, suspected of offenses against the authority of the King, the royal family, or the security of the state, could be arrested and kept in detention until the expiration of the law, at the end of the following legislative session.

The power to issue warrants was vested in "authorized persons," a category which the Ministry refused to clarify. Certain checks against the abuse of this power were provided by supervisory procedures within the ministries of police and justice. If a magistrate issued a warrant, he was to notify the prefect within twenty-four hours, and the prefect, in turn, was to notify the Minister of Police. In addition, the persons delivering the warrant (invariably the justices of the peace) were to issue within twenty-four hours a report to the *procureur* of the district court. He, in turn, would submit this information to the *procureur-général* of the nearest royal appeals court, and from there, the information would be transmitted to the Minister of Justice. These procedures would not guard individuals against arbitrary arrest, for the grounds of suspicion had ultimately to emerge from the very personal assessment of some functionary. However, they would establish the channels through which the Ministry could check on the number and whereabouts of suspects.

Where grounds did not exist for imprisonment suspects could be placed under surveillance. The nature of the surveillance envisaged had been described in a section of Napoleon's penal code.[40] Three kinds were possible: in the suspect's normal place of residence, in another commune within the same department, or in a commune outside. In all instances there were to be regular reports by the suspect to the mayor or police commissioner of the town and no travel without prior authorization.

The proposed law passed the Chamber of Deputies on October 23 without modification or amendment. There were 294 votes for the measure and 56 in opposition. The clearest voices in the op-

[40] See penal code, chapter III, book I.

position were those of Voyer d'Argenson and Royer-Collard.[41] Only the former had spoken directly against the need for the bill: existing conditions, he claimed, had not been shown by the government to require exceptional legislation and thus arbitrary detention could not be justified.[42] Royer-Collard, on the other hand, had argued not against the need for the bill but against its possible abuse by a multitude of functionaries.[43] Spokesmen for the ultra-royalist majority, like Hyde de Neuville, felt threatened by both lines of criticism. They reminded Hyde de Neuville of a dangerous side of the Enlightenment: "Let us banish chimerical fears. Experience has cruelly and sufficiently proven to us the danger of speculative ideas." [44] The law on administrative arrests was promulgated on October 29, 1815.

At the same time that the bill extending police powers of arrest on political grounds was submitted for the consideration of the Chamber a bill extending and clarifying the range of seditious acts punishable by the courts was also presented.[45] To the new deputies the definition of subversion in relevant portions of the penal code appeared lacking both in comprehensiveness and severity. Napoleon's penal code was of value only in reference to acts that incited revolt:

Whoever shall have provoked a rebellion either by discourses in public places or meetings, or by posted signs or by printed writings, shall be punished as guilty of rebellion. Where no re-

[41] The committee reported the bill without changes on October 21. Discussion was opened and closed on October 23. See *Archives Parlementaires,* XV, 91–93, 93–104.

[42] It was at this point that Voyer d'Argenson said: ". . . some people have wrenched my heart by announcing that Protestants have been massacred in the Midi . . . " He wanted an investigation of these "rumors," or at least a report by the Minister, but sentiment was overwhelmingly against both suggestions. He limited himself to proposing a special committee to meet with the Minister on the subject of security measures. See *Archives Parlementaires,* XV, 99.

[43] *Archives Parlementaires,* XV, 96–98.        [44] *Ibid.,* p. 99.

[45] The bill was presented by Barbé-Marbois, Minister of Justice, on October 16: *ibid.,* pp. 76–78. Barbé-Marbois had replaced Pasquier in September.

bellion shall have followed, the provocateur will be punished by imprisonment of at least six days, and up to one year.[46]

A new measure, written largely by Guizot,[47] widened the concept of sedition to include any speech or writings menacing the life, authority or person of the King or the life and person of other members of the royal family. The effect of this, however, was to bring under the jurisdiction of the courts, rather than the police, persons suspected of such offenses. In addition, at the suggestion of Barbé-Marbois, Minister of Justice, spreading of rumors affecting the maintenance of legitimate authority was also covered. The bill made indirect as well as direct provocations to rebellious acts punishable by law and offenders were to be judged in the courts of first instance. Penalties were to range from three months to five years of imprisonment.

The sedition bill presented to the Chamber of Deputies on October 16 was referred for discussion to a legislative committee of distinctive composition. Four of its nine members, Chifflet, Pardessus, Jolivet, and Cardonnel, had sat on the legislative committee that amended Richelieu's amnesty bill. This committee proceeded to make major revisions in the sedition bill, hoping to gain government approval for these changes.

When the committee reported the bill on October 24, the classification of certain seditious acts had been changed from misdemeanors to crimes thereby increasing the penalties they would incur.[48] No longer was imprisonment to vary from one month

---

[46] Article 217.

[47] See Charles Pouthas, *Guizot pendant le Restauration: préparation de l'homme d'Etat (1814–1830)* (Paris, 1923), p. 117. Pouthas traced the authorship of Guizot and Barbé-Marbois from the handwriting on the manuscript in A.N., BB[30]190. Guizot had been secretary-general in the Ministry of Justice under Pasquier and remained there under Barbé-Marbois.

[48] See *Archives Parlementaires*, XV, 106–110. E.-D. Pasquier, *Histoire de mon temps*, IV, 10–12, has surprisingly little to say about this committee's work beyond the fact that his enmity toward Villèle was born in work on this bill and that if Villèle had had his way, the bill would have been even more severe.

to five years; the top penalty was now deportation. In addition the condemned man might pay a fine as high as 3,000 francs.[49]

The modification which upgraded some seditious acts from misdemeanors to crimes had, as an undesired consequence, shifted offenders out of the jurisdiction of the courts of first instance, and into that of the royal assize courts, fewer in number and slower in procedure. Pasquier, as rapporteur, asserted that this jurisdiction would be tolerated only as a temporary expedient. Trial by jury, a feature of criminal procedure in the assize courts, was much too long a process to be appropriate in sedition cases. The committee which reported the bill asked for the re-establishment of the provost courts of the Old Regime. They would be a much more appropriate tribunal for sedition cases, since there the severest penalties could be meted out without either jury or appeal.[50]

The committee's modified sedition bill was presented for debate on October 27.[51] Despite the harsher penalties now provided for by the bill, Barbé-Marbois announced that the King accepted the proposal as amended. Moreover, the Minister recognized the legislative committee's concern for swifter justice by inserting a preamble to the bill. It noted that while there had been hope that the ordinary courts would be adequate for the judgment of suspects, there was a need for "simpler forms, severer penalties, and more rapid justice . . ." The preamble gave formal assurances that a proposal for the re-establishment of the provost courts would be made shortly.[52]

Demands from the floor by a few ardent royalists for even harsher penalties did not prevent passage of the bill. The deputy

---

Villèle was eventually made a member of this committee: Cf. the list of members, *Archives Parlementaires*, XV, 106, and 426.

[49] As a result of an amendment from the floor, the maximum fine was later raised to 20,000 francs. *Archives Parlementaires*, XV, 159.

[50] *Archives Parlementaires*, XV, 106–110.

[51] The discussion continued for three days: October 27, 28, and 30: *ibid.*, pp. 142–148, 148–158.

[52] *Ibid.*, p. 110.

Piet had suggested that where the crime was raising the tricolor, the penalty should be changed from deportation to death.[53] Humbert de Sesmaisons had wanted to be assured that those convicted would be deported outside the continent of Europe.[54] The Ultra majority, nevertheless, was satisfied with a measure whose text they had helped to dictate in legislative committee and the bill passed the Chamber of Deputies on October 30. Supported by a large majority in the Chamber of Peers, it was proclaimed law on November 9, 1815.

Shortly after this new sedition law was passed, the Minister of War introduced a bill to re-establish the provost courts. In so doing, the Ministry fulfilled its pledge to the majority in the Chamber of Deputies. The functioning of this institution was, of course, dependent on factors which the Chamber could not control. The successful legal implementation of a desired vengeance depended upon the appropriateness of the institution designated for the task, and the compliance of Ministers and functionaries. The provost courts, as we shall see, were not to fulfill the Chamber's hopes.

[53] *Ibid.*, pp. 143–144.
[54] *Ibid.*, p. 143.

# V

# THE PROVOST COURTS

The Charter of the First Restoration had guaranteed certain rights to accused persons by conserving the criminal procedure of the ordinary courts under the Empire. In the ordinary courts accused persons in criminal cases had the right to judgment by jury and in both civil and criminal cases the right to appeal judgment.[1] Certain courts were authorized, however, in which the jury played no role in criminal proceedings and in which the right of appeal was absent. The provost courts (*Cours prévôtales*) had functioned this way under the Old Regime and their revival was specifically provided for by the Charter.[2]

The provost courts had existed since the sixteenth century and 33 such courts (*Cours prévôtales de maréchaussée*) were abolished in the first months of the Revolution. Under the Old Regime these courts had had jurisdiction over common-law crimes committed in rural areas and on the highways. Among such offenses were vagrancy, counterfeiting, smuggling, and armed assault and robbery. Soldiers who had committed common-law crimes were also tried before them rather than before a strictly military tribunal. The provost, under the Old Regime, was an officer of the

[1] See Jacques Godechot, *Les institutions de la France sous la Révolution et l'Empire* (Paris, 1951), pp. 212, 416, 522, 533, 536–541. Juries were alien to the court procedure of the Old Regime. The grand jury system, introduced in 1791, had been abolished in 1808 but the petty jury continued to play a role in judging accused persons. See also Alphonse Bérenger, *De la justice criminelle en France* (Paris, 1818); Adhémar Esmein, *Histoire de la procédure criminelle en France* (Paris, 1882).

[2] Article 63 of the Charter of 1814.

rank of colonel, who combined his judicial and police duties with active military service. He had the right to make arrests, hear witnesses, accuse and convict. Sentence was carried out within twenty-four hours, without appeal.

The special courts were, in their procedure and function, the Empire's successors to the provost courts. The special courts had been created in 1808 to deal with deserters and, like the provost courts before them, also had jurisdiction over certain common-law crimes committed on the highways and in rural areas and certain crimes committed by soldiers. Vagrancy, counterfeiting, smuggling, and armed assault and robbery all came within their jurisdiction. These courts were established in each department and five civil magistrates sat with three army officers as judges. There was no jury nor could the judgment be appealed. Before indictment could be made, however, the Court of Cassation in Paris had to rule on the competence of the special court to handle the case before it.

Within the Ministry of War the special courts had come up for review under the First Restoration. The legislative commission of the Ministry of War had been asked on February 11, 1815 to give its opinion on the constitutionality of the special courts and the advisability of replacing them by revived provost courts.[3] The majority of the commission stood behind the special courts and against the provost courts, whose procedure they found lacking in adequate guarantees to the accused. Their conclusions were that the special courts were both constitutional and adequate. Only political reasons, they said, could dictate the re-establishment of the other jurisdiction:

If, for reasons that one may believe are political, one should wish to re-establish the title of the outmoded provost jurisdictions as a sort of bogey *(épouvantail)*, this title might be conferred on the special courts in place of their present title.[4]

[3] A.N., BB³⁰190(2), memo to the legislative commission, February 11, 1815.
[4] A.N., BB³⁰190(2), report on special courts, forwarded with letter of Dalmatia

The Minister of War, the Duke of Dalmatia, communicated this report to the Minister of Justice, Dambray, who was already contemplating the re-establishment of the provost courts for political reasons. The Minister of Justice indicated his intention to do so well before the Hundred Days:

The old organization of the provost jurisdictions would undoubtedly be unsuited to our customs, and would be out of harmony with our laws. However, these jurisdictions are susceptible to changes which would make them more appropriate to our present situation. Because of this fact, we are still undecided. When the work I am having done on this subject is completed, I shall communicate it to you promptly, Monsieur, and I hope that a good bill will result from this fruitful association of *lumières*.[5]

The dislocation brought on by the campaigns of the Hundred Days and the withdrawal of the French army south of the Loire in July 1815 had, of course, interrupted the functioning of the special courts. The military men who had formerly served as judges were called to duty elsewhere.[6] The difficulty in re-establishing these courts after the Hundred Days revived the issue of their constitutionality. While the Charter had authorized all existing jurisdictions, the special courts had nowhere been mentioned by name. In addition, the Charter had expressly forbidden the creation of any courts of exceptional procedure; only the provost courts were specifically excluded from this ruling.[7]

However, no more was heard of the plan to replace the special by the provost courts until well after Waterloo. In October, two days after the bill on seditious speech and writings had been

---

to Minister of Justice Dambray, March 1, 1815. Members of the legislative commission were Vignolle, Charpentier, Brenier, Besson, and Volland from the Ministry of War. They were joined by Le Graverend from the Ministry of Justice.

[5] A.N., BB$^{30}$190(2), Minister of Justice to Minister of War, March 2, 1815.

[6] See the speech of Barbé-Marbois to Blondel d'Aubers in the Chamber of Deputies on October 28, 1815. *Archives Parlementaires* (Paris, 1869), deuxième série, XV, 149.

[7] Cf. articles 59 and 63 of the Charter of 1814.

placed before the Chamber of Deputies, Barbé-Marbois, the new Minister of Justice, ordered the project revived:

A committee of magistrates will prepare, in the shortest time possible, a bill for the re-establishment of the provost jurisdictions, conforming as much as possible to our present law and jurisprudence.[8]

Convoked on October 21, the committee prepared a draft to submit to the Conseil d'Etat on October 25.[9] On November 17 the Duke of Feltre, Minister of War, read the bill to the Chamber of Deputies.[10] It was clear that the provost courts were now to have a role in the enforcement of the sedition law of November 9.

In presenting the bill the Minister of War noted that the provost jurisdiction had a long history of useful service dating from the sixteenth century and that the courts were neither revolutionary nor untried. Their major advantage, he said, was that, since the judge served as prosecutor and there was no appeal, trial could be speedy.

He pointed out that these courts were designed to replace the special courts and were an improvement over them. Procedure had been too slow in the special courts: the need for the Court of Cassation in Paris to judge the competence of the special court before the hearings could begin delayed the proceedings too much, particularly in areas far from the capital. Furthermore, the presence of three military men among the judges was used to poor advantage. They served as examining magistrates and rarely rendered final judgment. As a result their presence did not speed up the course of the trial appreciably.

[8] A.N., BB$^{30}$190(2), decree of October 18, 1815. Four members of the Conseil d'Etat, Portalis, Dudon, Royer-Collard and Séguier, met with two magistrates, Barril and Jacquinot, to prepare the bill.

[9] A.N., BB$^{30}$190(2), Barbé-Marbois to members of the committee, October 21, 1815 (copy); Dudon to Marbois, October 25, 1815.

[10] *Archives Parlementaires,* XV, 248–250. The Duke of Feltre became Minister of War on March 4, 1815, and followed Louis XVIII to Ghent.

Thus, according to the Minister, the new courts represented an improvement over both the provost courts as they had existed under the Old Regime and the special courts as they had functioned under the Empire. They would be more numerous than the old provost courts and quicker to present a verdict than the special courts. There would be one provost court in each department while there had been only thirty-three in all under the Old Regime. The determination of competence was to be vested in one of the numerous royal appeals courts, and hearings could begin in a case before a ruling had been made on the provost court's competence.

In the bill presented, the range of offenses over which the provost courts would have jurisdiction included not only the common-law crimes judged by its two predecessors but the more serious political offenses defined in the sedition law of November 9. Thus, the new provost courts would have competence over all speech and writings directly threatening the safety of the sovereign and the state, if they had been pronounced, posted, or distributed in a public place. The display of the tricolor, as described by the new sedition law, was also considered within their jurisdiction. In addition, of course, acts of armed rebellion as defined by the penal code came within their competence as they had within that of the special courts.

Meeting an anticipated criticism, the Duke of Feltre denied that the provost courts would institute a reign of terror. He wished to make clear that he did not consider the provost courts at all similar to the Revolutionary tribunals. The competence of the new courts would be limited to instances of public menace or manifest violence and they would not be involved in ferreting out secret plots. As an additional guarantee they would be staffed by men of good character, whose powers would be defined by rules of office:

A legitimate government can only view with horror anything

which might resemble, even from afar, those detestable tribunals [of the Red Terror], so worthy of their name. They covered our country with blood, during a period whose memory every Frenchman would like to forget.[11]

The bill was reported to the Chamber by its legislative committee on December 1, with only minor changes proposed.[12] These concerned largely the competence and procedure of the courts. The competence of the provost courts was to be limited in the case of common-law crimes to acts committed in areas where local police had no jurisdiction. No such territorial limit was to exist in the case of political offenses. The power of arrest, which the Minister's bill had limited to the provost and the police detail at the service of the courts, was extended in the committee's version to a variety of local officials and policemen. Another alteration, this time of symbolic significance, was the specification that those convicted of crimes calling for capital punishment die by hanging, rather than by the guillotine, instrument of the Revolution.

Discussion of the bill in the Chamber of Deputies opened on December 4. Duplessis de Grenedan, who had enrolled to speak in favor of the bill, instead criticized its terms.[13] He claimed that the provost courts to be set up were in excess of the number required. He also had some questions about the personnel who would staff the courts. The judges from the courts of first instance were "the refuge and source of mediocrity." Judges who had formerly condemned men to a maximum of five years in prison were not the ones best suited for work in tribunals where they would have the power to condemn a man to death without appeal. The speaker suggested that the proposed provost courts be reduced by two thirds in number, functioning only where there were royal assize courts, and that their personnel be drawn

[11] *Ibid.*, pp. 247–248.
[12] *Ibid.*; Cf. Feltre's bill, November 17, 1815, pp. 248–250.
[13] *Ibid.*, pp. 374 ff.

from the judges of those courts. With regard to criminal procedure he argued that one should not proceed to the accusation of the suspect before the competence of the court had been approved by a higher tribunal. "Haste to do justice is praiseworthy, but it should not carry us beyond the limits of reason and humanity."

Voyer d'Argenson, who had previously called attention to the plight of Protestants in the Gard, voiced his dissatisfaction with the trial procedure and the competence of the new courts. The government had failed to show the need for exceptional jurisdictions and the possibility of re-establishing the provost courts, opened up by the wording of the Charter, could hardly be considered a command to establish them. There was no need to dispense with the hard-won guarantee of jury trial. Furthermore, the proposed provost courts had a competence much greater than that of the provost courts under the Old Regime and the Charter did not sanction this extension of jurisdiction.[14]

Trinquelacque, who had sat on the legislative committee reporting the bill to the Chamber, improvised a defense of the bill on the ground that it was called for by public demand. Cuvier, as a delegate of the King supporting the government's proposal, answered the objections adroitly. By the afternoon of December 4 discussion on the committee's report had ended and the individual articles came up for a vote. The first eleven articles, largely concerned with organizational questions, were passed without amendment.

When the issue of defining the jurisdiction of the provost courts arose, the deputies Try and Murard de Saint-Romain wished to have their competence extended beyond the limits indicated in the proposed legislation. Try wanted to see the burning of mills, granges, and rural buildings come under the authority of the provost courts: "In the crisis in which we now find ourselves, these [acts] result from feelings of vengeance and hate

[14] *Ibid.*, pp. 376–378.

which must be severely repressed." Murard de Saint-Romain wished to see the theft of sacred vessels in the churches added to the list of crimes within the provost court's competence. Both amendments were rejected.[15]

Proposals to alter the trial procedure had some success. An amendment proposed by Duplessis de Grenedan was adopted, clearly denying the provost courts the right to proceed to accusation until their competence in a case had been confirmed by the royal assize court.[16] However, a motion by Hyde de Neuville for a sufficient delay in the carrying out of a death sentence to permit a royal pardon or commutation of sentence was defeated.

The bill passed the Chamber of Deputies much as it had emerged from the legislative committee. On December 4 it was read to the Chamber of Peers. The text of the bill was reported from a committee of the upper house on December 15 and adopted the same day. On December 20 it became law.

The actual establishment of the provost courts was a slow process. Few of the courts were functioning by the end of February. While the major population centers had provost courts by the end of April 1816, many departments were without them for a longer period. In the Southwest the provost court of Montauban was not installed until June and the court in Foix did not begin to function until September.[17] The result was that the courts had little opportunity to play a role in political cases before the end of the summer.

One reason for this delay lay in the procedure for appointing judges.[18] The tribunals could not begin to function until the Ministries of both War and Justice had appointed the magistrates. The Minister of War was to nominate one provost to each of 86 departments. The law had specified that the candidates

[15] *Ibid.,* p. 379.

[16] *Ibid.,* p. 390.

[17] For the dates of installation in the Southwest, see Henri Ramet, "Les cours prévôtales dans le ressort de la Cour d'appel de Toulouse," *Recueil de l'Académie de Législation de Toulouse,* VIII (1929), quatrième série, pp. 13–14.

[18] See BB³175, Dossier 1, memo of February 20, 1816.

have at least the rank of colonel. However, given the variety of military services performed by émigrés and the difficulty of checking out their records, it was impossible to carry out this ruling faithfully and still proceed with any speed. Ultimately many candidates were accepted with very little deliberation. As a confidential ministerial source described the process:

The bureau of military justice submitted to the Duke of Feltre a list of officers who were soliciting the favor of nomination as provosts and whose services had not been at all verified. The Duke approved the nomination of some of the officers included there and substituted some names for others. This list, endorsed with the signature of the Duke of Feltre, was sent to the Minister of Justice without any other verification, and made the subject of a decree. It was thus that the law of December 20, 1815, which specified that provosts be taken from among the military or naval officers with at least the rank of colonel was carried out.[19]

If the Ministry of War was confronted with a mass of applicants whose qualifications could not be certified, the Ministry of Justice was faced with a simple shortage of eligible candidates. In both instances problems of staffing created delays. Five civil magistrates were to be chosen by the Minister of Justice from among the judges of the court of first instance in the city in which the provost court was to be located. At the time these choices were to be made, however, the personnel of the courts of first instance, like that of the assize courts, had been reduced by the voluntary withdrawal of some magistrates and the purge of others.[20] This purge had been made possible by a decision of the Ministry to grant tenure initially only to judges who had been appointed by the King.[21]

[19] Archives de Guerre, C¹⁸58, report of July 18, 1818. See also lists of provosts nominated, A.N., BB³175.

[20] Perhaps one third to one half of the magistrates had been purged. See Charles Pouthas, *Guizot pendant la Restauration* (Paris, 1923), p. 126.

[21] See Paul Bastid, *Les institutions politiques de la monarchie parlementaire*

Some of the cities in which the provost courts were to be established were also the sites of royal appeals courts. In these centers the problem of recruiting judges from the lower courts for the provost courts was all the greater. Since many of the magistrates in the appeals courts heard cases in the lower ones as well, the nearby court of first instance was often understaffed. Thus, according to a ministerial source, one-third of 27 cities having a royal appeals court had no more than four of the five required magistrates sitting on their courts of first instance. To take them away for duty in the provost courts would have meant suspending the process of hearing, accusation, and judgment in the lower courts. This was the situation in Aix where delay was caused by understandable unwillingness to suspend such operations. In this case efforts were finally made to recruit magistrates from lower courts in other cities of the department, contrary to the specifications of the law.[22]

Once organized the provost courts continued to be an administrative problem.[23] One reason was that the provosts, new to their role as judges, were often unaware of the precise limits placed on their powers. This was in some instances due to the absence of necessary information. There is evidence, as in a request from the provost of the court at Dijon, that the military judges were not being sent copies of the *Bulletin des Lois,* and that some of the new provosts did not have copies of the laws of November 9, 1815 and December 20, 1815.[24] They were thus without precise knowledge either of the competence assigned their tribunals or of the laws which they were expected to apply.

_____

*française (1814–1848)* (Paris, 1954), pp. 345–346, for an analysis of the constitutional issue.

[22] See A.N., BB³175, Dossier 4, for a Ministry of Justice memo, without date, dealing with this problem. Four of the civil magistrates were to serve as judges and one as a president of the provost court.

[23] See BB³123, 124, 125, 126, for a voluminous correspondence. A circular from the Minister of Justice to the provosts, March 23, 1816, complains about the number of requests being addressed directly to the Minister: BB³175. This carton also contains correspondence with the provost.

[24] A.N., BB³126, Provost of Côte d'Or to Minister of Justice, June 7, 1815.

Jurisdiction in political cases was initially determined by the gravity of the offense. If the seditious act was committed in a public place and involved a direct threat to the security of the King or the state, it went before the provost courts. When the threat was indirect, it went before the courts of first instance. There was considerable latitude in determining the nature of an oral or written imprecation. The cry "A bas le Roi" was most often understood as a direct menace to the life of the King, and hence as a crime, to be judged by the provost courts. "Vive l'Empereur" was an offense likely to be judged by the ordinary courts as a misdemeanor.

The competence of the provost courts for political offenses was generally determined by the decision of either the judges of the provost court or that of the *procureur-général* in the nearest royal assize court. In these decisions the jurisdiction of the ordinary courts was usually favored over that of the provost courts. This was clearly the case when the magistrates of the provost court (most of them judges from the court of first instance) had to decide whether a suspect detained as a result of a warrant issued by the provost court should be tried by that court.

The judges of first instance realized that the provost court was only a temporary institution. Moreover, they could not have wished to weaken the authority of the ordinary courts from which they were drawn, and to which they would return later on a full-time basis.[25] Thus, in the Seine and in the Seine-Inférieure, the judges on the provost court interpreted the jurisdiction of that court very narrowly by refusing to acknowledge competence over a seditious act which had not been committed in a truly public place.[26] Similarly, in the Basses-Alpes the judges of the provost court denied their competence in a case of sedi-

[25] See the interesting speculations on this subject by Jean Vidalenc, "La cour prévôtale des Bouches-du-Rhône (1815–1817)," *Congrès des Sociétés Savantes de Paris et des départements* (Toulouse, 1953), section d'histoire moderne et contemporaine, pp. 285–293. The records in BB³123 are his only source, however.

[26] A.N., BB³125, court records.

tious speech because the Emperor had been invoked only in an indirect fashion.[27] An examination of the register of the ordinary courts in the Côte d'Or reveals numerous cases which might just as easily have been placed within the jurisdiction of the provost court.[28]

Similar decisions were made by the *procureurs-généraux* of the royal assize courts in assigning cases to the appropriate tribunals. They seemed to favor the courts of first instance over the provost courts, and expected the Minister of Justice to support this policy. Thus, the *procureur-général* in Dijon protested to the Minister of Justice when the provost of the Saône-et-Loire exceeded his authority by proceeding against individuals who had been accused of putting up Bonapartist posters, and against others who had been accused of interfering with the transport or sale of grain. The *procureur-général* considered these as borderline cases that did not belong in the competence of the provost court and the Minister of Justice agreed. His reply read as follows: "In doubtful cases, it is prudent to send the suspects before the ordinary judges." [29]

Those provosts who showed a great zeal in their efforts to bring more cases under their own jurisdictions came into conflict with the Ministers of Justice and War. The exchange with the provost of the Seine illuminates this problem.[30] Maréchal de Camp de Messey found that his staff was inadequate to carry out the responsibilities assigned to him by the law. In order to go to the area of disturbance in cases of "flagrant crime" or "public out-

[27] A.N., BB³123, court records.
[28] Ferdinand Claudon, "La Cour prévôtale de la Côte d'Or (1816–1818)," *Bulletin du Comité des travaux historiques* (Paris, 1924), X (1924), Section histoire moderne et contemporaine, pp. 131–132. This is the only study that has compared the activity of the two courts in political cases on the basis of records of operation in the same district.
[29] A.N., BB³126, Minister of Justice to Provost of Chalons-sur-Saône, July 5, 1816.
[30] See A.N., BB³126, provost de Messey to Minister of Justice, January 26, 1816, March 2, 1816; Minister of War to Minister of Justice, February 5, 1816; reply of Minister of Justice to letter of March 2, 1816, no date.

cry," as specified by the law, he needed an adequate police force to make arrests and a clerical staff to take notes on the testimony of witnesses. For this purpose he had only the clerical staff and police detail assigned to the court of first instance and none of his own. In a letter sent under separate cover to the Minister of Police, the Minister of Justice, and the Minister of War, he asked for sufficient funds to create a special police force under his orders and an administrative staff that could go through the reports of the gendarmerie to check independently on which cases were in the competence of his court. The Minister of Justice reminded him that he had no right to initiate complaints against individuals and cautioned him to contain his zeal.

With little knowledge of such internal problems, it was easy for liberal critics of the period to exaggerate the role played by the provost courts. The fact that a military figure served as judge and that the ordinary procedural guarantees were much reduced encouraged critics of the regime to imagine the worst. The few major cases in which the death penalty had been prescribed were considered as representative of sentences meted out generally for the more serious political offenses and the provost courts shared an infamous reputation. Thus Achille de Vaulabelle wrote of the beginnings of the Second Restoration:

There was not a citizen who, in scanning a newspaper, could not read a summary of those numerous political trials which succeeded one another during more than a year, either in the assize courts, before the military tribunals, or in the provost courts. The ordinary outcome of these trials was the death sentence.[31]

In the absence of a public statement from the Ministry of Justice rumors had grown about the number of political offenses being handled by the provost courts. Alphonse Bérenger, a noted jurist writing in 1818, had estimated the number of persons con-

[31] A. de Vaulabelle, *Histoire des Deux Restaurations,* 2nd ed. (Paris, 1847), IV, 107.

demned for political offenses in the previous two and a half years at 9,000 persons and he in no way minimized the contribution of the provost courts to this total.[32] Nevertheless, the unpublished results of a ministerial inquiry in the same year indicated that the provost courts had not played the role in judging political offenders hoped for by their supporters in the Chamber of Deputies or imagined by their critics.

In a circular of February 20, 1818, the Minister of Justice, Pasquier,[33] requested a report from the provost courts on the cases that had come under their jurisdiction since their establishment. A statement by the King in November 1817 had indicated that the life of the courts would not be extended by legislative act during that session and that an analysis of their activity was desired before their dissolution. The reports that were returned provide the basis for the description here.[34]

Of a total of 2,280 cases that came before the provost courts in two years of activity no more than 265 can be considered political in nature. Approximately 1,560 concern only the common-law offenses which had earlier been within the jurisdiction of the special courts.[35] The great majority of the political offenses were described by the sedition law of November 9, 1815. In this category were 237 cases involving seditious speeches or writings, and the display of the tricolor. An additional 28 cases of a political nature may be found among the offenses classified as "armed rebellion" and "seditious assembly."

---

[32] A. Bérenger, De la justice criminelle en France (Paris, 1818), p. 590. This figure was also offered by Henry Houssaye, 1815, 50 ed. (Paris, 1911), p. 594, as an estimate of the number of political cases dealt with by the provost courts and other competent tribunals.

[33] Pasquier had returned to the Ministry of Justice in January 1817.

[34] See A.N., BB³123, 124, 125, 126, and below, explanatory note to the Appendix.

[35] The small number of political offenses dealt with by the provost courts was first pointed out by André Paillet, "Les cours prévôtales," Revue des Deux Mondes, IV (1911), sixième période, pp. 123–149, through a tally of the cases described in A.N., BB³123, 124, 125, and 126. My own tally of the number of specifically political cases dealt with by the courts agrees with his. See A. Paillet, "Les cours prévôtales," p. 140, for the common-law offenses.

Armed rebellion is deceptive as a classification for it did not necessarily signify political protest. There were 243 cases classified in court records as "armed rebellion," 173 as "seditious assembly," and 65 as "murder by armed bands" or "attempted murder." An examination of these archives indicates that with the exception of 28 cases which represented a specifically political protest, the rest were most often economic in nature. They included resistance to tax collectors, attempts to lower the price of grain or prevent its shipment, and collective efforts to cut wood in public forests.[36]

Contraband was a major problem in some of the frontier departments. In the Nord, 110 of the 164 cases which came before the provost courts had to do with contraband and armed rebellion against the customs officers.[37] The provost court in the Moselle, which handled 82 cases, had 36 which dealt in some way with customs offenses.[38] Twenty-four of 33 cases that came before the provost court in the Ardennes were of this character.[39] This frontier was unusually active, however, and no similar activity was reported along the Spanish border.[40]

The records of the provost courts do not indicate an unusually high incidence of crimes of violence in the South as a whole although some individual departments had a relatively high incidence of such cases. In the Bouches-du-Rhône 18 of the 37 cases handled by the provost court involved armed robbery and armed assault.[41] In the Var there were 36 such cases out of 61.[42]

[36] For a discussion of attempts to control the price of grain and prevent its shipment in 1816–17, see Robert Marjolin, "Troubles provoqués en France par la disette de 1816–17," *Revue d'histoire moderne,* VIII (1933), 423–460.
[37] A.N., BB³123, court records.
[38] See A.N., BB³124, tables and letters from procureur of Moselle to Minister of Justice, March 16, 1818 and April 26, 1818.
[39] A.N., BB³123, court records.
[40] See A.N., BB³124, court records. In the Basses-Pyrénées, the court handled 24 cases, of which only 2 were for smuggling. The Hautes-Pyrénées handled only 7 cases, of which one was for armed rebellion against a customs officer. The Pyrénées-Orientales had 16 cases, of which at least 5 involved contraband. The Ariège and the Haute-Garonne list no cases specifically involving smuggling.
[41] A.N., BB³123, court records.
[42] A.N., BB³125, court records.

In the Gard only 17 cases were handled, of which 11 were for armed robbery, assault, and murder. In the Haute-Garonne 43 cases were dealt with, but most involved conflicts with public officials over the price and shipment of grain or the appropriation of wood from the public forests.[43] In the Vaucluse and the Basses-Alpes only 25 cases of all kinds came within the competence of the two provost courts.[44]

The provost courts rarely imposed penalties of deportation or death for political offenses.[45] However the penalty was often more severe than warranted by the gravity of the offense. Furthermore the same offense might be prosecuted in quite different ways in different departments. A parody of the Lord's Prayer circulated in the Haute-Garonne without any individuals being brought before the provost court for prosecution.[46] In the Côte d'Or, however, a peasant was sentenced to deportation for passing a similar parody to a neighbor in the market of Auxonne:

Notre père qui êtes aux Tuileries, que votre règne cesse, que votre volonté soit sans effet sur la terre, comme dans le ciel. Pardonnez-nous nos victoires, comme nous pardonnons la lâcheté de votre noblesse, et ne nous conduisez pas à la tentation de vous détrôner, et pour cela délivrez-nous de votre présence. Ainsi soit-il.[47]

In the fewer than 300 cases of a political character that came before the provost courts the judges rarely imposed the severest penalty which the offense would permit. In most political cases

---

[43] A.N., BB³123, court records.

[44] A.N., BB³125, court records. A. Paillet, "Les cours prévôtales," p. 141, cites the example of the Vaucluse as an area of abnormal criminal activity, but though the record for the provost court's activity in the department lists 6 cases of assault, and one involving murder, there were a total of only 11 cases examined. The Basses-Alpes handled 14 cases.

[45] The imposition of 11 death sentences in the Affaire de Lyons, June 1817, was an unusual act by a provost court.

[46] H. Ramet, "Les cours prévôtales dans le ressort de la Cour d'appel de Toulouse," p. 37.

[47] Quoted in F. Claudon, "La Cour prévôtale de la Côte d'Or," p. 142.

the judges used the option given them to impose milder penalties when they found in hearing a case that it could be classified as a simple misdemeanor.[48] Thus, though the prison sentence in most political cases was more than three years, it usually did not exceed five years. These penalties were, nevertheless, heavier than those meted out by the ordinary courts for similar offenses.[49]

Authorized only in December of 1815 the provost courts were created slowly in the course of succeeding months. Because they were established late and functioned badly the provost courts had but a small role in the political reaction of 1815–16. Instead the bulk of the political convictions in 1815–16 were made by the ordinary courts. When there was not enough evidence to prosecute, action was often taken by the police under the special powers of detention granted by the law on administrative arrests. The ordinary courts and the police, though drawing less attention than the *Cours prévôtales,* were the effective instruments of the Bourbon reaction.

[48] See article sixteen of the law of December 20, 1815, creating the provost courts.

[49] See the discussion of penalties imposed by the ordinary courts for such offenses in the following chapter.

# VI

## POLITICAL ARRESTS

## AND CONVICTIONS

The judicial reforms of the Revolution had not been able to eliminate permanently the "lettre de cachet," which reappeared in a new guise under the Consulate and Empire. The power of the government to detain suspects arbitrarily had been increased under Napoleon in three successive measures. First, the Constitution of the Year VIII (1799) had given the government the right to arrest persons suspected of plotting against the security of the state. Such persons could be detained for ten days before being surrendered to the courts. As a second step, a Senate ruling of 1802 gave that body the right to determine for itself, without reference to the Consular Constitution, the moment when suspects would be brought to trial. Finally, an imperial decree of March 3, 1810, ended the prospect of eventual trial and established a category of administrative arrests.[1]

Those detained for political reasons under the Empire had usually been kept in a separate category of fortress prisons. These included Mont Saint-Michel, Vincennes, the Chateau d'If, and Saumur. Only when the fortresses became full did the imperial

---

[1] Political suspects, held incommunicado in one of the state prisons or forced to live among common criminals in an ordinary jail, numbered about 2,500 in the last months of the Empire. See Jacques Godechot, *Les institutions de la France sous la Révolution et l'Empire* (Paris, 1951) pp. 542–543, and footnotes pp. 536–537 for references.

regime place its enemies in the ordinary prisons used by the courts. Unlike the prisons which usually held persons sentenced by the courts or awaiting sentence, those for detained political suspects were not under the general supervision of the *procureurs-généraux* of the appeals courts but rather under that of the prefects. However, the prefects exercised little real control over these prisons, since inspection of the fortresses depended on annual visits by certain specially designated members of the Conseil d'Etat. If, upon inspection, the gravity of the charges brought against prisoners was found insufficient to justify continued confinement, suspects might be sent to some rural community to remain under the surveillance of the local police.

The First Restoration inherited the police powers and prisons of the Empire but, in the spirit of conciliation then dominant, these powers were used very little against supporters of the Revolutionary and Napoleonic regimes. Arbitrary measures were employed again by Napoleon during the Hundred Days but for the surveillance of political suspects rather than their detention in prisons. A three-man commission in each department, composed of the military commander, the *procureur* of the court of first instance, and the prefect had drawn up from their separate sources of information a list of persons suspected of plotting against the security of the state. Where there were no grounds for action by the courts, such suspects had been placed under surveillance in distant departments.[2]

This policy of restraint in the exercise of police powers during the Hundred Days was expressed by Fouché in instructions to the prefects:

We must abandon the errors of that *police d'attaque* which, continually stirred up by suspicion, continually disturbed and turbulent, threatens without guaranteeing [safety] and torments

[2] See, for example, A.D.H.G., 4M34, Decree of March 23, 1815.

without assuring protection. We must contain ourselves within the limits of a liberal and positive police, of that *police d'observation* . . . calm in its efforts, measured in its pursuits . . .[3]

The dominant ministerial attitude toward the use of the police remained the same at the beginning of the Second Restoration when Pasquier became Interim Minister of Interior and Justice. It was expressed in a circular sent out by Barante to the prefects on July 17, 1815:

It is by never deviating from the constitutional line which the government of the King is following, in being ceaselessly absorbed with all the details of your office, in paying attention to the way your business is conducted, in carrying out an exact and satisfactory justice for all, that you may quiet certain exasperated and disturbed minds. The support and the individual advantages that each person will receive from a regime of liberty and from regular administration are the best and even the only means of conciliation among all parties.[4]

Away from Paris, however, the departmental administrations were willing, at the beginning of the Second Restoration, to associate themselves with a variety of arrests for political reasons. In some instances this involved the normalization of a detention initiated by the action of royalist gangs immediately after the Liberation. However, the prefects of only fourteen departments had reported themselves responsible for the detention of political suspects before the passage of the law of October 29.[5] One hun-

---

[3] A.D. Gard, 6M22, Fouché to prefects, March 31, 1815. See also E.-D. de Pasquier, *Histoire de mon temps: Mémoires du Chancelier Pasquier* (Paris, 1894), III, 186 (footnote), who stresses the opposition within Napoleon's entourage to measures of repression.

[4] A.D. Hérault, 4M52, Barante to prefects, Circular No. 2, July 17, 1815.

[5] Arrests made before October 29 are indicated by a superscript *b* following the November entries in Table 2 of the Appendix. The tabulation was made from information given by the prefects when they submitted reports on persons in their departments affected by the law of October 29, 1815. See A.N., F⁷9880 and

dred and one persons were the object of those measures.[6] The grounds for the arrests made before October often violated the promise of the Charter to forget all opinions and acts prior to the Restoration. The report on three men arrested between July 21 and October 14 in Toulouse read as follows: "Very suspect because of excesses committed during the Revolution." [7] Each spent from two to five months in prison and was then placed under surveillance.

Minister of Police Fouché tried to limit unauthorized arrests under the Second Restoration as he had during the Hundred Days. He did not approve the vagueness of accusations which brought some persons into custody. The following remark appeared in the summary of correspondence with the prefects on September 15:

The subprefect of les Andelys (Eure) has had two harvesters arrested as suspected of "having wished to arrest the progress of public opinion." The prefect is invited to remind his administrators that under a constitutional regime it is still necessary to avoid the vagueness and odiousness of accusations and to put one's self on guard against a too easy resort to arbitrary acts.[8]

Ultra-royalists hoped that Elie Decazes, Fouché's successor as Minister of Police, despite his record of service under the Empire, would be more willing to employ the power of arrest in political cases. The instructions which he was to send out to the

F⁷9881 for those reports, which cover the period from November 1815 through December 1817. They have been tabulated for the monthly incidence by department in Table 2, and further information about the nature of the reports is given in the explanatory note to the Appendix.

[6] The breakdown by departments was as follows: Aveyron, 2; Creuse, 7; Doubs, 3; Drôme, 2; Eure, 2; Haute-Garonne, 3; Gard, 22; Jura, 30; Loire-Inférieure, 7; Pyrénées-Orientales, 13; Bas-Rhin, 1; Haut-Rhin, 1; Vaucluse, 5; Yonne, 3.

[7] A.N., F⁷9881, dossier Haute-Garonne.

[8] A.N., F⁷3786, Bulletin de Police, September 15, 1815. This was probably Fouché's last bulletin as Minister.

prefects on the implementation of the law of October 29 would greatly influence the law's impact. During debate on the bill Decazes had refused to indicate how the new powers would be interpreted.[9] His first eagerly-awaited instructions, issued a few days after the promulgation of the law, were a great disappointment to the Duke of Angoulême and to those in the Chamber of Deputies who hoped the new law would authorize an extended wave of arrests.[10]

Decazes' circular of November 1 defined narrowly the circumstances in which the power of detention was to be applied and specified the officials who were to exercise it. The power of detention was limited to the examining magistrates, who usually issued warrants of arrest, to the prefects of the departments and to the prefect of police in Paris. At the same time Decazes tried to avoid the abuse of those powers by specifying that they were intended as a supplement and not an alternative to those exercised by the courts:

It [the law of October 29, 1815] intended to indicate that it is not on the basis of simple suspicions or vague denunciations that one should deprive a citizen of his liberty. The powers it grants should only be applied when the insufficiency and not the absence of proof prevents the case from being brought before the courts.

The ministerial circular called for monthly reports from the prefects on the use they were making of this power.[11]

Had it not been for the broad interpretation given to the law

[9] See above, Chapter IV, pp. 77–78, and the speech of Royer-Collard in the Chamber of Deputies on October 23, 1815, *Archives Parlementaires* (Paris, 1869), deuxième série, XV, pp. 96–98. Royer-Collard had spoken eloquently about the dangers of the law granting arrest power indiscriminately to a host of functionaries.

[10] A.N., F⁷9877, Decazes to prefects, November 1, 1815. Angoulême found that this circular had destroyed much of the good effect of the law; see Archives Priveés, Papiers Vaublanc, Angoulême to Vaublanc, n.d. [November 7?, 1815].

[11] These reports, in A.N., F⁷9880 and 9881 supplied the information for Table 2.

by the recently appointed Minister of the Interior, Vaublanc, it would have affected only a few hundred persons rather than several thousand. Vaublanc, a friend of the ultra-royalists, maintained communication with the Duke of Angoulême, and like the Minister of Police, was in correspondence with the prefects. On October 28 he expressed his point of view to the prefect Chabrol in Lyons:

The law on prolonged detention will be approved: do not be concerned about this. The Ministry, the Chambers, and the King will approve your actions and if necessary I will make myself responsible for you. By striking the rebellious by sudden arrests you will break the web of their conspiracies, you will strike fear into them, you will prevent the slaughtering of royalists, and you will draw a much larger part of the national guard behind you by making them act than if you asked of them only passive service.[12]

The law of October 29, in line with Vaublanc's hopes, gave rise to new arrests. As Table 2 of the Appendix indicates, 39 departments which had not reported the application of such measures earlier reported arrests of political suspects in November. Measures were taken against 318 persons in that month and 229 persons in December. By the end of December only 21 departments had not invoked the law, and a total of 648 persons were reported affected.[13]

By the end of January 1816 only the Cher, the Corrèze, the Haute-Vienne, the Lot, the Ardennes, the Haute-Saône, the Moselle, and the Basses-Alpes had no administrative arrests to report. The number of persons affected by the law continued to

[12] Archives Priveées, Papiers Vaublanc, Vaublanc to Chabrol (draft), October 28, 1815. A copy was sent to Angoulême.

[13] Table 2 of our Appendix, compiled from manuscript sources, indicates that only 14 departments, marked by a superscript *b,* reported arrests of political suspects before passage of this law. For the monthly incidence of arrests, see Table 2.

rise. Measures were reported against 377 persons in January, and against 428 more in February. In March, however, the monthly totals began to drop.

The trend downward was interrupted in May. An increase of two to seven times the activity of the preceding month was reported in most departments. The activity was particularly heavy in the Isère and neighboring areas. Arrests in the Isère went from 6 in April to 75 in May; in the Ain from 1 in April to 24 in May; in the Jura from 1 to 21 in the same period. In the Côte d'Or there had been 14 arrests in April and there were 57 in May. In the Drôme the number rose from 1 in April to 17 in May. The Basses-Alpes reported its only 3 arrests during May.

The explanation for the new wave of arrests in that area is to be found in the Didier conspiracy at Grenoble in May 1816, an event of local significance. Jean-Paul Didier of the Faculty of Law in Grenoble gathered a thousand peasants and soldiers to march on the city on May 4. His partisans never entered the gates, however, for General Donnadieu's troops fired on them, killing six and dispersing the rest. Didier claimed to have had contacts with the Duke of Orléans but his own statement of a tenuous connection remains the only evidence for such a tie. Most of the participants believed the coup was being staged in favor of Marie-Louise and Napoleon II. A military commission and the provost court joined in the suppression of the revolt and there were 16 executions in two days.[14]

Persons affected by the police measures in May were those whose past behavior had led royalists to believe they might become involved in a new conspiracy related to the Didier affair. If there had been real evidence of conspiracy, however, the sus-

[14] See A.N., BB³123 for the action taken by the Provost Court of the Isère; Henry Dumolard, *Jean-Paul Didier et la conspiration de Grenoble, 4 mai, 1816; La Terreur Blanche dans l'Isère* (Grenoble, 1928), esp. chapter viii. It may have been the repression of this uprising that made Stendhal say that the White Terror in Grenoble was worse than the Red Terror: Henri Beyle, *Vie de Henry Brulard* (Paris, 1949), édition Henri Martineau, I, 133.

pects could have been brought before the courts. In Brioude (Haute-Loire), the tenuous grounds for arresting one man were described as follows:

Very outspoken on March 20 [1815] in behalf of the Usurper; recognized as one of the principal exalters of suspicious hopes . . . [He] was being carefully watched without any apparent measures having been taken against him but at the time of the events in Grenoble we feared his influence in case of trouble . . . [15]

A report from Breteuil in the Oise tells of a traveling blacksmith who was placed under surveillance on May 28:

He was traveling through the countryside shortly after the affair of Grenoble in order to spread alarming news. Despite the lack of positive proof against him, the prefect believed it was his duty to place him under surveillance because of the danger of his opinions.[16]

Although arrests were often made on a very slight pretext, suspects usually found that the period of prison detention was quickly terminated in favor of some form of surveillance. This usually involved a personal appearance before the *commissaire de police* once or twice a week; in some cases it entailed a daily visit.[17] It also meant that permission was required from the competent authorities, usually the mayor or the *commissaire de police,* before the suspect could spend a night away from his commune.

Sixty to seventy-five percent of those affected by the law of October 29 were released shortly after arrest and placed under a regime of surveillance. All but a few of the others were released

---

[15] A.N., F⁷9881, dossier Haute-Loire.

[16] A.N., F⁷9881, dossier Oise.

[17] Registers of surveillance note their visits. See, for example, the register in the Archives Municipales de Toulouse, I², 6.

for surveillance within five months. For this purpose, the individual suspect was usually allowed to remain in his ordinary place of residence. In a list of 2,609 persons affected by the law, two thirds were described as under surveillance in their home towns; the rest, with the exception of those kept in jail, had been sent to other communes, not always in the same department.[18]

Those suspects detained in the jails had a difficult time and the unhealthy conditions in the prisons were not the only hazard.[19] Once in prison it was extremely difficult to obtain one's release. The correspondence of the industrialist Boyer-Fonfrède illustrates the exasperation and frustration of the prisoner. He had written from his cell:

If the laws had been adhered to in my case, the existence of a few pounds of powder for hunting in my home would not have served as a pretext for a new persecution. . .

I do not know on what grounds I have been treated as a state criminal for sixty-two days, when it is agreed that there are no grounds for court proceedings.[20]

Former office-holders, most often of the Hundred Days, appear frequently on the police lists of those affected by the law on administrative arrests.[21] Their detention or surveillance outside their own commune was undoubtedly connected with local feuds and initially with the purge of office-holders in progress. In

---

[18] See A.N., F⁷9877, report of June 19, 1816, for this figure. My own tally for political arrests made under the law, as of June 1, 1816, is 2756 persons, and can be made from the figures presented in Table 2. For a description of the sources drawn on, see the explanatory note to the Appendix.

[19] See the very revealing report on the state of the prisons by Le Graverend in A.N., BB³⁰254, April 13, 1816.

[20] A.D.H.G., 4M36, Boyer-Fonfrède to prefect of Haute-Garonne, October 17, 1815. Boyer-Fonfrède, however, had been president of the Confédération du Midi during the Hundred Days. See J.J. Hémardinquer, "Affaires et politiques sous la monarchie censitaire; un libéral: F.-B. Boyer-Fonfrède (1767–1845)," *Annales du Midi*, LXXIII (1961), 165–218.

[21] See A.N., F⁷9880 and 9881, and see explanatory note to Appendix for further information about the nature of these lists.

central France 15 of 54 persons arrested in the department of the Indre before the end of 1816 were former office-holders. Two primary school teachers, a number of court officials, a tax-collector and an inspector general of forests were in this group. Similarly, in the department of the Nièvre, 23 of 66 persons arrested between November 1815 and December 1816 were former office-holders. They included two former tax-collectors, four former mayors, three former primary school teachers, a few minor court officers, and assorted police officials.

In the South, 17 of the 113 persons affected by the law in the department of the Tarn were former office-holders. In this group were five former mayors, the former police commissioner of Castres, a former subprefect, the *procureur-général* of the royal court in Toulouse, as well as the perennial tax-collector. In the West, a total of 20 persons in the department of the Vendée had been affected by the law before the end of 1816. In this group, three were former office-holders, two were former mayors, and one was a former tax-collector.[22]

A second group frequently affected by the law were the discharged soldiers and the *demi-solde*.[23] In the Vendée and the Haute-Loire, they were as numerous as the former office-holders, comprising 10 out of a list of 72 persons in the former and 3 out of 20 in the latter. Elsewhere their representation was less important. In the Nièvre there were but 6 men in this category out of 66 under arrest or surveillance by the end of 1816.[24]

Through the period from November 1815 to the end of 1816 "married priests" and "former priests" appear as a small but still persistent element in the list of persons affected by the law. It was a rare department that did not show at least one former priest on its list of arrests and surveillance. In the Haute-Loire

---

[22] See A.N., F⁷9881, dossiers Indre, Nièvre, Tarn, Vendée, Haute-Loire.

[23] Jean Vidalenc, *Les demi-solde: Etude d'une catégorie sociale* (Paris, 1955), offers a good reconstruction of the life of these former officers under the Restoration. He finds that they generally avoided political involvement.

[24] See A.N., F⁷9881, dossiers Haute-Loire, Vendée, Nièvre.

the case of Vialard is described. He had held a job in Le Puy and was sent back for a period of surveillance to his native commune in the neighboring department of the Ardèche. The justification for this decision on April 6, 1816 read as follows: "Suspected of being a leader of the anarchist party; much immorality and daring." [25] More specific charges were levied against Honoré Bastie, a former priest living in Marrevaux in the Basses-Pyrénées, arrested on March 12, 1816. The statement about him reads as follows:

Renegade priest, [he] once played in the Revolutionary comedy entitled "Le dernier jugement des Rois," poor political opinions, partisan of the Usurper, bad subject, suspected of carrying on a criminal correspondence with suspect persons.[26]

During this entire period the ordinary courts were actually playing a more active role in dealing with political suspects than were the police. Even before the law of November 9 was passed there had been a limited number of convictions for subversive acts under the provisions of the penal code concerned with various forms of rebellion.[27] As indicated in Table 1 of the Appendix, 41 departments had reported that a total of 296 convictions had been made in the ordinary courts between July and September 1815 for political offenses.[28]

A wide range of subversive acts during the Second Restoration could be punished by a new application of relevant articles of the penal code. Thus, the court at Saint Marcellin in the Isère sentenced an apprentice to ten days in prison for having in July

[25] See A.N., F⁷9881, dossier Haute-Loire.
[26] See A.N., F⁷9881, dossier Basses-Pyrénées.
[27] Articles 76, 77, 86, 91, and 102 of the penal code were all relevant. See also articles 100, 212, 217, 219, and 222. Articles 52, 100, 222, and 479 were cited by courts of first instance in the departments of the Yonne and the Haute-Garonne in August 1815.
[28] To make this tabulation, see the data presented in Appendix, Table 1, July–September 1815.

"worn a shako embellished with insignia of the rebellion." [29] In the town of Clamecy in the Nièvre a field hand who had formerly been a soldier was sentenced to six days in prison by the court for "having worn a tricolor emblem in his hat on August 23 in the marketplace." [30] At Lavaur in the Tarn, a 55-year-old mason was sentenced to two months in prison for answering the "Qui vive?" of a sentry with "Républicain." Before the same court, two farmers and an iron forger were given sentences of one month to a year for having cried out: "Vive l'Empereur; Merde pour le Roi." [31]

As a result of new sedition legislation penalties for political offenses were increased. The typical prison sentences imposed for political offenses under Napoleon's penal code had been mild, ranging from five or six days to an occasional six months. The maximum jail sentence that could be imposed for inciting a rebellion without success was a term of one year. Sentences were rarely appealed. Occasionally, a zealous *procureur-général* initiated a review of the sentences of a court of first instance whose penalties he considered too mild. The appeals court usually confirmed the earlier sentence.[32] With the passage of the law of November 9, 1815, however, the penalties for such acts became more severe. The minimum jail sentence for unsuccessful provocations to rebellion was raised from six days to three months and the maximum from one year to five years.

Thereafter, too, the number of departments reporting convictions in political cases increased considerably. A total of 1885 convictions in political cases was reported for the last three months of 1815, a sixfold increase over the preceding three-month period.[33] Although passage of the law cannot be given

[29] A.N., F⁷9997, dossier Isère.
[30] A.N., F⁷9997, dossier Nièvre.
[31] A.N., F⁷9997, dossier Tarn.
[32] This was true in a number of cases reviewed by the appeals court of Toulouse in the autumn of 1815: see A.N., F⁷9994, dossier Haute-Garonne.
[33] Compare the two trimester totals for 1815 tabulated in Appendix, Table

credit for the entire increase, which was in part a function of a greater total activity of the courts, the new law did provide an instrument for extending the reaction.

An examination of official records indicates that police powers of detention were most often used when the courts hesitated to apply the new sedition law against political suspects. Thus, in most departments, the number of political suspects arrested as an administrative measure varied inversely with the number actually sentenced by the courts. Given the procedure by which many political arrests were made this relationship is understandable. When the examining magistrate did not consider the evidence sufficient to bring a political suspect to trial, or when a suspect was released after trial, the examining magistrate would frequently alert the police so that administrative measures could be imposed.

Many illustrations of this cooperative relationship can be found. Thus, along the frontier with Spain, the Basses-Pyrénées, the Hautes-Pyrénées, and the Pyrénées-Orientales, which had an incidence of political arrests above the median in November and December of 1815, and throughout the following year, had an incidence of court convictions for political offenses below the median. Similarly, in the Bouches-du-Rhône, the Vaucluse, and the Isère, where administrative arrests were above the median in the last three months of 1815, court convictions were below the median for the same period. This was also the case in the Center, for the departments of the Aveyron, the Haute-Loire, the Creuse, the Nièvre, the Yonne, and the Loire; in the East for the Meuse and the Bas-Rhin; and in the North for the departments of the Pas-de-Calais and the Nord. In the Drôme, the Puy-de-Dôme, the Seine-et-Oise and the Marne, where the number of convictions was above the median, the number of arrests fell below it.[34]

---

1. Seventy-one departments reported convictions after the law of November 9, 1815, went into effect. Only 41 had reported convictions earlier.

[34] The median number of court convictions for political offenses in the third

In certain areas however, the incidence of both administrative arrests and court convictions in political cases was above the median. This was true in the Southwest, for the departments of the Charente-Inférieure (Maritime), the Charente, and the Gironde, as it was for the Haute-Garonne and the Tarn-et-Garonne. In the South the same held true for the Gard, the Hérault, the Tarn, and the Aude. Similarly, in the East and Southeast, the Jura, Doubs, Rhône, and Ain were areas in which both arrests and convictions registered above the median. The same was true in the Parisian region and the Northwest for the Seine-et-Marne, the Seine, and the Seine-Maritime. It is unfortunate that the records examined are not complete for the departments of the West some of which may also belong in this category.[35]

Almost every department of France was affected to some degree by the legal reaction that began in the late fall of 1815 and lasted through the following year. Nevertheless, the areas identified above as centers of the reaction in its legal phase had an incidence of both arrests and convictions out of proportion to the population of the departments concerned. Only 6 of the 16 departments noted as having an incidence of both administrative arrests and court action above the median in political cases had a population larger than the departmental average.[36] Of the 15 most populous departments, only 3 had an incidence of administrative arrests and

and fourth quarters of 1815 was 30. Those departments that registered 51 or more convictions for that period fall into the top quartile. Through December 1815 the median number of arrests of political suspects in the 85 departments was between 3 and 4. Those departments with an incidence of 8 or more arrests are in the top quartile. By the end of 1816 the median of total arrests per department had risen to 26. Those departments in the top quartile at the end of that year had made 44 or more arrests.

[35] The departments for which court records are missing in the F[7] series are indicated in the explanatory note to the Appendix. Political arrests in the Ille-et-Vilaine, the Sarthe and the Orne were above the median, but not in Deux-Sèvres or Maine-et-Loire.

[36] On the basis of the 1821 population census, indicated in Table 1 of the Appendix, the average department was one with a population of approximately 356,000 persons. The six departments noted above were the Seine, Seine-Inférieure, Gironde, Charente-Inférieure, Haute-Garonne, and Rhône.

court convictions above the median, although 11 were above the median in arrests alone.[37] Six of 9 departments in the South and Southwest having an incidence of both arrests and convictions above the median were of less than average population.[38] The materials of local history will need to be examined further for an explanation of the variations in this incidence of the legal reaction, as they have been for the incidence of the White Terror the preceding summer.

The combined records of the courts and the police now allow us to assess the magnitude of the "legal Terror" of 1815–16, and to revise substantially earlier estimates. Available information from 61 percent of the trimester court records indicates that from the beginning of July 1815 to the end of June 1816, 3,746 persons were sentenced by the ordinary courts for political offenses.[39] This figure is raised to a total of about 6,000 convictions if we compensate for missing data by projections based on average court activity for known departments in the same period. A calculation of this kind yields a figure one third lower than the widely accepted estimate of 9,000 convictions in political cases.[40]

The information gathered from official police records demands a more drastic revision of the most frequently pronounced estimate of arrests during the period of the White Terror. The source for this estimate was Achille de Vaulabelle. Hostile to the legitimist cause and writing more than 30 years after the Terror,

[37] The fifteen most populous departments, in descending order, were the Nord, Seine, Seine-Inférieure, Pas-de-Calais, Manche, Puy-de-Dôme, Côtes-du-Nord, Ille-et-Vilaine, Gironde, Somme, Isère, Bas-Rhin, Saône-et-Loire, Calvados and Aisne.

[38] Those six departments were the Gard, Hérault, Aude, Tarn, Tarn-et-Garonne and Charente.

[39] See explanatory note and Table 1 in the Appendix.

[40] As far as I can determine, this estimate first appeared in Alphonse Bérenger, De la justice criminelle en France (Paris, 1818), p. 590. It reappeared in Henry Houssaye, 1815, 50th ed. (Paris, 1911), p. 594, and more recently in Paul Bastid, Les institutions politiques de la monarchie parlementaire française (1814–1848), (Paris, 1954), p. 346. G. de Bertier de Sauvigny, La Restauration (Paris, 1955), p. 181, tried to establish an estimate independently, but research had not yet brought to light enough relevant data. In a later edition, La Restauration, 2nd ed. rev. (Paris, 1964), p. 133, he was able to integrate my findings.

Vaulabelle alleged in his history of the Restoration that there had been 70,000 arrests "in the last months of 1815 and the first eight months of 1816."[41] This would have meant an average of a little over 800 arrests for each department. Since official records indicate that three quarters of the departments had less than 100 authorized arrests and no evidence of others by royalist bands during July and August of 1815, Vaulabelle's figure seems improbable. It would have meant that in the remaining departments of France there had been an average of 2,000 to 3,000 arrests. This figure may possibly have been attained in the departments of the Gard, Haute-Garonne, and Bouches-du-Rhône, for reasons discussed in the first part of this study but there is no evidence of a comparable reaction elsewhere. Vaulabelle may simply have used these atypical departments to project the incidence of arrests for the country as a whole. Given Vaulabelle's authority, and the absence of conflicting estimates, the willingness of other historians to refer to his view of the magnitude of the White Terror has been understandable.[42]

From November of 1815 through the following February the law of October 29 was frequently invoked in police arrests. Yet in none of those months did the law affect more than 500 persons. The curve of arrests did rise again at the moment of the Didier uprising in May but only briefly. Thereafter the number of persons affected by the law continued to dwindle. Through the months of October, November, and December 1816 no more than 100 persons were reported the object of police measures for political reasons in the entire country. By the time that Louis XVIII gathered the courage to dissolve the Ultra Chamber of Deputies in September 1816 the fever of the political reaction was spent.

[41] A. de Vaulabelle, *Histoire des Deux Restaurations* (Paris, 1847), IV, 96–97.

[42] Although critical of this figure as an exaggeration, Professor Charles Pouthas has presented it for the reader's consideration. See his postwar Sorbonne lectures, "Histoire politique de la Restauration" (Paris, n.d.), mimeographed, p. 43, and the skepticism registered earlier in *Guizot pendant la Restauration* (Paris, 1923), p. 119.

# VII

# CONCLUSION

---

Ernest Daudet's study of the Terror, first published in 1878, has long influenced our view of what transpired in the summer of 1815. With limited access to archival materials, then neither well ordered nor easily consulted, Daudet was content to recount a series of violent episodes without investigating either the relationship between them or the parties responsible. Criminal elements commit crimes, he argued, and "all parties have committed errors." [1] The need for tolerance was the major lesson he wished to offer to his readers in the early years of the Third Republic. In his study he denied that any specific responsibility for the climate of terror in the Southwest could be traced to ultra-royalist political leadership.

My own conclusion has been that events like the murder of General Ramel, the intimidation of Protestants in Bas Languedoc, and the hunting-down of political suspects in Marseilles, each had their place in an ultra-royalist attempt to seize and maintain power in the summer of 1815. The representatives of the Duke of Angoulême came into positions of authority in Provence and Languedoc with the liberation of those provinces and they remained in power through the second week in August. During this period the worst excesses were committed. They were condoned and sometimes encouraged by the Chevaliers de la Foi and the royalist committees with which Angoulême's government

[1] Ernest Daudet, *La Terreur Blanche* (Paris, 1906), p. xiii.

collaborated. By condoning arrests, extortion, intimidation, and violence, the new royalist authorities helped to assure themselves the continuing support of their most militant and least disciplined partisans. What is more, the excesses of the Terror drove Napoleon's officials into hiding and created a power vacuum which the Duke's representatives could fill.

The Duke's appointment of Ultras to public office in the South, and his defense of their right to hold those offices, expressed a militant disapproval of the policies and personnel of the moderate Ministry in Paris. Some members of the Ministry mistook his secessionist tactics for secessionist goals. Evidence of their error may be seen in the support Angoulême gave to government centralized in Paris once his own special powers were revoked. That support was completely consistent with the preference he had indicated earlier for Napoleon's system of administration.

It is probably true that some members of the ultra-royalist leadership in Toulouse wished to make Angoulême's government of the Midi a center of authority for a secessionist South, a new "Kingdom of Aquitaine" as Charles de Rémusat described it. In a letter to the Director of the Archives in 1877, cited here for the first time, Ernest Daudet indicated his private belief that this was true:

Family papers and oral testimony have furnished me proof that the ultra-royalist party in Toulouse wanted . . . to detach the Midi from France and that her leaders had premeditated the murder of Ramel. I did not say so [in my book].[2]

My own research has indicated that responsibility for the murder probably rested with a small subgroup within a local cell of the Chevaliers de la Foi and that this action was taken to widen the

[2] See A.N., Dossier de travail 21606ᴬ, Ernest Daudet to Directeur général des archives, November 3, 1877. I would like to thank the staff of the National Archives for the cooperation which made the discovery of this letter possible.

gulf between the central government and local royalist extremists. However, the murder of Ramel took place in Angoulême's absence and before it was known in Toulouse that Angoulême's powers had been revoked. It was not intended as a step on the road to secession.

An explanation for the evaporation of separatist sentiment may be found in the success of the ultra-royalist leadership in its quest for public office. In the purge of office-holders in 1815–16, many more people were affected than had been touched by the private vengeance of the preceding summer or the action of the police and the courts thereafter. Fifty to eighty thousand job-holders, a quarter to a third of those on government payrolls, were dismissed from their posts.[3] There was hardly a branch of government, civil or military, local or national, that was not affected in some way by these changes. No comparable purge had taken place during the First Restoration or during the Hundred Days and none to compare with this would take place before the Revolution of 1830.

Where the punishment of alleged Bonapartists was concerned the Ultras enjoyed a more limited success. During the summer of 1815 royalist bands in southern France placed hundreds of persons in jails, and perhaps 200 to 300 civilians were assassinated. Several thousand persons from the cities of Marseilles, Toulon, and Nîmes were forced into hiding. During succeeding months, after the passage of repressive legislation, about 6,000 persons were affected by court sentences and more than 3,000 by police action. In magnitude the White Terror was greatly overshadowed by the Red Terror of 1793–94. During the earlier Terror about 17,000 people were sentenced to death by the courts.[4]

[3] This is the estimate offered by G. de Bertier de Sauvigny, *La Restauration* (Paris, 1956), p. 182. For the evidence of a purge at the departmental level, on which this projection is based in part, see, by the same author, "F. de Bertier, Préfet du Calvados," *Bulletin de la Société des Antiquaires de Normandie* (1959), pp. 226–261. More studies of this kind are needed to improve our estimate of the purge.

[4] See Donald Greer, *The Incidence of the Terror during the French Revolution: A Statistical Interpretation* (Cambridge, Mass., 1935), pp. 26, 37, and tables.

# CONCLUSION

It is hardly surprising that the White Terror failed to attain the dimensions of the Red. The conditions of peace and military occupation in 1815–16 discouraged a violent security hysteria and the Bourbon government in Paris restrained rather than impelled the search for subversives. The first Ministry of the Second Restoration represented continuity with the revolutionary and imperial past and was responsive to demand from within and without France for internal peace and stability. Control over the administration, the police, and the courts belonged to them, and the Ultra legislature had only a limited power to make the laws. The effect of ministerial action was to cripple the Ultras in their efforts to limit the amnesty, expand the definition of sedition, and increase the powers of special courts.

Despite the fact that repressive legislation was not more effectively implemented, the experience of ultra-royalists in putting through a legislative program was a significant one. Out of a growing sense of their own strength in the legislature, the Ultras gave unexpected support to the development of parliamentary government. In the course of their struggle against recalcitrant ministers, Ultras in the Chamber brought under discussion the issue of ministerial responsibility so ambiguously defined in the Charter. The wrath which these ultra-royalists had earlier turned against the governmental system created by the Charter of 1814 was safely channeled into criticism of specific ministers. Although the fight for the responsibility of the Ministry to the Chamber of Deputies was later taken up by constitutional moderates in a war against the Ultra ministers of Charles X, the Ultra deputies of 1815–16 deserve credit for beginning the battle. In so doing they contributed greatly to refining the parliamentary process in France.

Nevertheless, in their denial of the spirit and letter of the Charter—through a limitation of the amnesty, support for arbitrary arrest, and curbs on free speech—Ultras indicated a very conditional loyalty to nineteenth-century constitutionalism. As arrests and convictions began to wane Ultras became convinced that their repressive measures had been successful in ending criticism of the government. In reality, as one must conclude from the records of the police and judiciary, there had been no organized opposition to the Bourbons. Without a clearly recognizable enemy, the reaction gradually lost its impetus in the cumbersome administrative machinery of government.

Mistaken in their judgment that the Terror had helped to stabilize the regime, the Ultras were to follow the course of reaction in succeeding periods of crisis. After the assassination of the Duke of Berry, and again after opposition developed to the Polignac Ministry, Ultras responded by curtailing guarantees of individual liberty. In so doing, they left the defense of the Charter to the revolutionaries of 1830. The inevitable result of this abandonment of the principles of the Charter was to associate closely legitimism with reaction and to widen the gulf between the House of Bourbon and the French nation.

# APPENDIX

# APPENDIX

---

The data used to make up Table 1 on the political activity of the ordinary courts come from dossiers in F⁷9993–9997 at the Archives Nationales. Each court of first instance and each court of appeals, in conformity to article 600 of the criminal code, submitted to both the Minister of Justice and the Minister of Police a quarterly report of the cases that had come before it. Reports were submitted in the form of a digest of the log kept by the clerks of each court. The cartons F⁷9993–9997 contain the digests which were sent to the Minister of Police in 1815 and 1816.

The form for each digest established columns under which the name, age, profession, and domicile of the suspect were listed, along with other relevant information. Specifically called for were a brief description of the alleged violation of the law, the dates when the case was considered, the action taken, the appeal if any, and additional observations the court clerk might wish to make. Not all court clerks supplied the required information in each column, but in almost all cases more than enough information was given to allow classification of a case as political or nonpolitical.

The decision whether to consider a particular case political was my own. It was determined by the nature of the offense as described in the record, the opinion of the judges, and the statutes invoked. Wherever the law of November 9, 1815 was invoked by the judges to establish their authority in a case, I have considered the case political in nature. Prior to the passage of this law, the courts saw authority for an attack on seditious speech and writings in relevant articles of Napoleon's penal code.

Cartons F⁷9993-9997 contain reports on the activity of the ordinary courts in the last six months of 1815 from 72 of 85 departments in mainland France (Corsica has not been considered). Missing for this six-month period are reports from nine departments—Calvados, Manche, Orne, Marne, Meuse, Vosges, Maine-et-Loire, Mayenne, and Sarthe. For four others, Côte d'Or, Loire, Saône-et-Loire, and Haute-Marne, one of two trimester reports is absent. The reports of only 30 departments could be found for the first six months of 1816. Dashes indicate missing reports.

Data on the activity of provost courts are drawn from the dossiers submitted by provosts shortly before the dissolution of the courts in 1818. These records are to be found in cartons BB³123, 124, 125 and 126 at the Archives Nationales. Information on cases handled was submitted on a form, an *Etat général,* which provided separate columns for information about the suspect, the circumstances of the arrest, the offense of which the suspect was accused, and the action taken.

Here again, the decision about which cases were to be considered political was my own, and was based on the description of the case given in the *Etat général* and the particular legislation invoked by the judges in establishing their competence. There is no evidence that the majority of attacks on customs officers, forest guards, tax-collectors, gendarmes and like authorities were political in character. In most cases, such attacks were simply auxiliary to the execution of crimes like smuggling, poaching, and tax evasion, even though they fell in the category of armed rebellion.

In order to allow the reader to assess the incidence of convictions in relation to population, the table offers in its second column the population of each department to the nearest thousand, as of the census of 1821. Of the more reliable censuses made after the Napoleonic wars, this one is closest in time to the period of the White Terror.

The information given in Table 2 was compiled from reports submitted to the Minister of Police by the prefects of 85 departments (Corsica has been excluded), and none are missing. They may be found in the Archives Nationales, cartons F⁷9880 and 9881. The reports were responses to a circular of the Minister of Police requesting knowledge about how the law of October 29, 1815 had been implemented. Submitted, for the most part, between September and

November of 1816, with supplements arriving later, they followed a form suggested by the Ministry. Information was given first about the name, profession, place of origin, and residence of the suspect. This was followed, in other columns provided for that purpose, by a description of the measures taken against the suspect, the reasons for them, and the source of authorization. On the basis of this information, ministerial aides in Paris kept a cumulative record of the monthly incidence by department. I have given combined totals by department, region, and the country as a whole for activity in November and December of 1815, the 12 months of 1816, and the entire 14-month period. Such totals are not given in cartons $F^7 9880$ and 9881, but there are two *Etats numériques* in $F^7 9887$ which are clearly ministerial efforts to tabulate the number of arrests reported by prefects from all departments. One *Etat*, dated June 19, 1816, does not break down the incidence by months, but lists a total of 2609 persons affected by the law. Another, without date, carries totals on a monthly basis through the end of November 1816. It lists 3326 persons affected by the law. This is 56 short of the figure I have independently calculated on the basis of monthly activity reported in $F^7 9880$ and 9881. That total is calculated for the 14-month period in Table 2.

Table 1. Convictions in political cases

| Departments[a] | Population to nearest 1,000[b] | Ordinary courts | | | | | | | Provost courts 1816–1818 |
|---|---|---|---|---|---|---|---|---|---|
| | | July–Sept. 1815 | Oct.–Dec. 1815 | Total | Jan.–Mar. 1816 | Apr.–June 1816 | Total | Total twelve months | |
| Paris (Seine) | 822 | 8 | 45 | 53 | — | — | — | 53 | 24 |
| Parisian Region | | | | | | | | | |
| Aisne | 460 | 0 | 7 | 7 | 13 | 17 | 30 | 37 | 3 |
| Aube | 231 | 7 | 22 | 29 | 23 | 19 | 42 | 71 | 3 |
| Eure-et-Loir | 264 | 0 | 19 | 19 | 17 | 12 | 29 | 48 | 0 |
| Loiret | 291 | 0 | 20 | 20 | — | — | — | 20 | 0 |
| Oise | 376 | 3 | 24 | 27 | — | — | — | 27 | 0 |
| Seine-et-Marne | 303 | 8 | 27 | 35 | — | — | — | 35 | 9 |
| Seine-et-Oise | 425 | 14 | 35 | 49 | — | — | — | 49 | 10 |
| Totals | 2350 | 32 | 154 | 186 | 53 | 48 | 101 | 287 | 25 |
| Northwest | | | | | | | | | |
| Calvados | 493 | — | — | — | — | — | — | — | 5 |
| Eure | 416 | 7 | 30 | 37 | 37 | 20 | 57 | 94 | 1 |
| Manche | 594 | — | — | — | — | — | — | — | 7 |
| Orne | 423 | — | — | — | — | — | — | — | 1 |
| Seine-Inférieure | 656 | 38 | 59 | 97 | — | — | — | 97 | 7 |
| Totals | 2582 | 45 | 89 | 134 | 37 | 20 | 57 | 191 | 21 |

(Table 1 continued)

| Departments[a] | Population to nearest 1,000[b] | Ordinary courts | | | | | | | Provost courts 1816–1818 |
| --- | --- | --- | --- | --- | --- | --- | --- | --- | --- |
| | | July–Sept. 1815 | Oct.–Dec. 1815 | Total | Jan.–Mar. 1816 | Apr.–June 1816 | Total | Total twelve months | |
| **Center** | | | | | | | | | |
| Allier | 280 | 0 | 18 | 18 | 17 | 11 | 28 | 46 | 0 |
| Cantal | 252 | 0 | 5 | 5 | 6 | 10 | 16 | 21 | 1 |
| Cher | 240 | 1 | 16 | 17 | 17 | 12 | 29 | 46 | 0 |
| Corrèze | 273 | 0 | 18 | 18 | 17 | 20 | 37 | 55 | 0 |
| Côte d'Or | 358 | 12 | — | 12 | — | — | — | 12 | 7 |
| Creuse | 249 | 0 | 16 | 16 | 15 | 5 | 20 | 36 | 0 |
| Haute-Loire | 277 | 1 | 15 | 16 | — | — | — | 16 | 4 |
| Haute-Vienne | 272 | 0 | 14 | 14 | — | — | — | 14 | 5 |
| Indre | 230 | 0 | 14 | 14 | 12 | 9 | 21 | 35 | 0 |
| Indre-et-Loir | 282 | 3 | 30 | 33 | 22 | 22 | 44 | 77 | 0 |
| Loir-et-Cher | 228 | 15 | 52 | 67 | — | — | — | 67 | 1 |
| Lot | 275 | 0 | 11 | 11 | — | — | — | 11 | 0 |
| Nièvre | 258 | 1 | 15 | 16 | — | — | — | 16 | 4 |
| Puy-de-Dôme | 553 | 0 | 98 | 98 | — | — | — | 98 | 1 |
| Yonne | 333 | 2 | 23 | 25 | — | — | — | 25 | 10 |
| *Totals* | 4360 | 35 | 345 | 380 | 106 | 89 | 195 | 575 | 33 |

(Table 1 continued)

| Departments[a] | Population to nearest 1,000[b] | Ordinary courts | | | | | | | Provost courts 1816–1818 |
|---|---|---|---|---|---|---|---|---|---|
| | | July–Sept. 1815 | Oct.–Dec. 1815 | Total | Jan.–Mar. 1816 | Apr.–June 1816 | Total | Total twelve months | |
| **North** | | | | | | | | | |
| Nord | 906 | 1 | 18 | 19 | — | — | — | 19 | 3 |
| Pas-de-Calais | 627 | 3 | 22 | 25 | — | — | — | 25 | 10 |
| Somme | 509 | 2 | 4 | 6 | — | — | — | 6 | 2 |
| *Totals* | 2042 | 6 | 44 | 50 | — | — | — | 50 | 15 |
| **South** | | | | | | | | | |
| Ardèche | 304 | 8 | 17 | 25 | 23 | 20 | 43 | 68 | 0 |
| Aude | 253 | 6 | 97 | 103 | 52 | 30 | 82 | 185 | 7 |
| Bouches-du-Rhône | 314 | 0 | 12 | 12 | — | — | — | 12 | 1 |
| Gard | 334 | 10 | 44 | 54 | 56 | 44 | 100 | 154 | 1 |
| Hérault | 324 | 4 | 49 | 53 | 34 | 48 | 82 | 135 | 10 |
| Lozère | 134 | 0 | 7 | 7 | — | — | — | 7 | 0 |
| Pyrénées-Orientales | 143 | 2 | 10 | 12 | — | — | — | 12 | 1 |
| Tarn | 314 | 17 | 88 | 105 | — | — | — | 105 | 6 |
| *Totals* | 2120 | 47 | 324 | 371 | 165 | 142 | 307 | 678 | 26 |

128

(Table 1 continued)

| Departments[a] | Population to nearest 1,000[b] | Ordinary courts | | | | | | Total twelve months | Provost courts 1816–1818 |
|---|---|---|---|---|---|---|---|---|---|
| | | July–Sept. 1815 | Oct.–Dec. 1815 | Total | Jan.–Mar. 1816 | Apr.–June 1816 | Total | | |
| Southeast | | | | | | | | | |
| Ain | 329 | 3 | 49 | 52 | 41 | 35 | 76 | 128 | 0 |
| Basses-Alpes | 149 | 0 | 5 | 5 | — | 3 | 3 | 8 | 2 |
| Drôme | 274 | 5 | 34 | 39 | 33 | 20 | 53 | 92 | 1 |
| Hautes-Alpes | 121 | 0 | 5 | 5 | 5 | 1 | 6 | 11 | 0 |
| Isère | 506 | 2 | 23 | 25 | 58 | 31 | 89 | 114 | 8 |
| Loire | 343 | — | 28 | 28 | — | — | — | 28 | 0 |
| Rhône | 391 | 0 | 45 | 45 | — | — | — | 45 | 0 |
| Saône-et-Loire | 498 | 9 | — | 9 | — | — | — | 9 | 10 |
| Var | 305 | 0 | 30 | 30 | — | — | — | 30 | 6 |
| Vaucluse | 224 | 0 | 13 | 13 | — | — | — | 13 | 0 |
| Totals | 3140 | 19 | 232 | 251 | 137 | 90 | 227 | 478 | 27 |

(Table 1 continued)

| Departments[a] | Population to nearest 1,000[b] | Ordinary courts | | | | | | | Provost courts 1816–1818 |
|---|---|---|---|---|---|---|---|---|---|
| | | July–Sept. 1815 | Oct.–Dec. 1815 | Total | Jan.–Mar. 1816 | Apr.–June 1816 | Total | Total twelve months | |
| East | | | | | | | | | |
| Ardennes | 267 | 4 | 0 | 4 | 9 | 17 | 26 | 30 | 1 |
| Bas-Rhin | 503 | 3 | 20 | 23 | — | — | — | 23 | 1 |
| Doubs | 243 | 6 | 43 | 49 | 38 | 21 | 59 | 108 | 0 |
| Haute-Marne | 233 | 6 | — | 6 | — | — | — | 6 | 1 |
| Haut-Rhin | 370 | 0 | 11 | 11 | — | — | — | 11 | 0 |
| Haute-Saône | 308 | 0 | 26 | 26 | — | — | — | 26 | 1 |
| Jura | 302 | 3 | 35 | 38 | 25 | 41 | 66 | 104 | 3 |
| Marne | 307 | 15 | 41 | 56 | — | — | — | 56 | 9 |
| Meurthe | 380 | — | — | — | — | — | — | — | 1 |
| Meuse | 291 | — | — | — | — | — | — | — | — |
| Moselle | 376 | 0 | 12 | 12 | — | — | — | 12 | 6 |
| Vosges | 358 | — | — | — | — | — | — | — | 0 |
| Totals | 3938 | 37 | 188 | 225 | 72 | 79 | 151 | 376 | 23 |

(Table 1 continued)

| Departments[a] | Population to nearest 1,000[b] | Ordinary courts | | | | | | | Provost courts 1816–1818 |
|---|---|---|---|---|---|---|---|---|---|
| | | July–Sept. 1815 | Oct.–Dec. 1815 | Total | Jan.–Mar. 1816 | Apr.–June 1816 | Total | Total twelve months | |
| West | | | | | | | | | |
| Charente | 348 | 12 | 30 | 42 | 19 | 17 | 36 | 78 | 0 |
| Charente-Inférieure | 409 | 0 | 32 | 32 | 39 | 30 | 69 | 101 | 6 |
| Côtes-du-Nord | 552 | 4 | 16 | 20 | 32 | 20 | 52 | 72 | 1 |
| Deux-Sèvres | 280 | 0 | 21 | 21 | — | — | — | 21 | — |
| Finistère | 483 | 0 | 9 | 9 | 15 | 23 | 38 | 47 | 5 |
| Ille-et-Vilaine | 533 | 3 | 27 | 30 | 28 | 41 | 69 | 99 | 11 |
| Loire-Inférieure | 434 | 0 | 9 | 9 | — | — | — | 9 | 4 |
| Maine-et-Loire | 443 | — | — | — | — | — | — | — | 2 |
| Mayenne | 344 | — | — | — | — | — | — | — | 0 |
| Morbihan | 416 | 4 | 7 | 11 | — | — | — | 11 | 5 |
| Sarthe | 428 | — | — | — | — | — | — | — | 5 |
| Vendée | 317 | 0 | 13 | 13 | — | — | — | 13 | 3 |
| Vienne | 261 | 0 | 14 | 14 | — | — | — | 14 | 3 |
| _Totals_ | 5248 | 23 | 178 | 201 | 133 | 131 | 264 | 465 | 45 |

131

(Table I continued)

| Departments[a] | Population to nearest 1,000[b] | Ordinary Courts | | | | | | Total twelve months | Provost courts 1816–1818 |
|---|---|---|---|---|---|---|---|---|---|
| | | July–Sept. 1815 | Oct.–Dec. 1815 | Total | Jan.–Mar. 1816 | Apr.–June 1816 | Total | | |
| Southwest | | | | | | | | | |
| Ariège | 235 | 9 | 43 | 52 | 14 | — | 14 | 66 | 0 |
| Aveyron | 339 | 0 | 15 | 15 | 13 | 16 | 29 | 44 | 5 |
| Basses-Pyrénées | 399 | 0 | 2 | 2 | — | — | — | 2 | 3 |
| Dordogne | 453 | 0 | 17 | 17 | 42 | 28 | 70 | 87 | 5 |
| Gers | 301 | 1 | 1 | 2 | 9 | 14 | 23 | 25 | 0 |
| Gironde | 522 | 1 | 37 | 38 | 39 | 34 | 73 | 111 | 5 |
| Haute-Garonne | 391 | 16 | 108 | 124 | 54 | — | 54 | 178 | 3 |
| Hautes-Pyrénées | 212 | 0 | 6 | 6 | — | — | — | 6 | 0 |
| Landes | 256 | 0 | 4 | 4 | — | — | — | 4 | 0 |
| Lot-et-Garonne | 330 | 0 | 21 | 21 | — | — | — | 21 | 1 |
| Tarn-et-Garonne | 238 | 17 | 32 | 49 | — | — | — | 49 | 4 |
| *Totals* | 3676 | 44 | 286 | 330 | 171 | 92 | 263 | 593 | 26 |
| *Final Totals* | 30278 | 296 | 1885 | 2181 | 874 | 691 | 1565 | 3746 | 265 |

[a] Corsica omitted
[b] 1821 census
— information lacking

Table 2. Arrests and surveillance of political suspects

| Departments[a] | 1815 | | | 1816 | | | | | | | | | | | Total fourteen months |
|---|---|---|---|---|---|---|---|---|---|---|---|---|---|---|---|
| | Nov. | Dec. | Total | Jan. | Feb. | Mar. | Apr. | May | June | July | Aug. | Sept. | Oct. to Dec. | Total | |
| Paris (Seine) | 58 | 34 | 92 | 68 | 51 | 17 | 21 | 87 | 31 | 17 | 46 | 13 | 51 | 402 | 494 |
| Parisian Region | | | | | | | | | | | | | | | |
| Aisne | 0 | 1 | 1 | 0 | 1 | 0 | 1 | 0 | 0 | 1 | 0 | 0 | 0 | 3 | 4 |
| Aube | 3 | 1 | 4 | 4 | 5 | 0 | 0 | 6 | 0 | 0 | 0 | 0 | 0 | 15 | 19 |
| Eure-et-Loir | 0 | 0 | 0 | 3 | 0 | 3 | 2 | 2 | 0 | 0 | 0 | 0 | 0 | 10 | 10 |
| Loiret | 8 | 10 | 18 | 4 | 2 | 3 | 1 | 1 | 2 | 0 | 0 | 0 | 0 | 13 | 31 |
| Oise | 6 | 3 | 9 | 2 | 1 | 2 | 2 | 9 | 0 | 1 | 0 | 0 | 0 | 17 | 26 |
| Seine-et-Marne | 4 | 5 | 9 | 5 | 5 | 1 | 4 | 2 | 0 | 2 | 31 | 0 | 0 | 50 | 59 |
| Seine-et-Oise | 1 | 0 | 1 | 5 | 1 | 5 | 0 | 3 | 1 | 0 | 0 | 0 | 0 | 15 | 16 |
| Totals | 22 | 20 | 42 | 23 | 15 | 14 | 10 | 23 | 3 | 4 | 31 | 0 | 0 | 123 | 165 |
| Northwest | | | | | | | | | | | | | | | |
| Calvados | 0 | 0 | 0 | 4 | 0 | 5 | 0 | 7 | 0 | 3 | 0 | 0 | 0 | 19 | 19 |
| Eure | 2[b] | 3 | 5 | 1 | 3 | 4 | 1 | 6 | 4 | 0 | 0 | 0 | 0 | 19 | 24 |
| Manche | 3 | 1 | 4 | 4 | 8 | 1 | 3 | 3 | 0 | 0 | 0 | 0 | 0 | 19 | 23 |
| Orne | 4 | 1 | 5 | 1 | 4 | 8 | 5 | 4 | 2 | 2 | 0 | 0 | 1 | 27 | 32 |
| Seine-Inférieure | 2 | 3 | 5 | 4 | 5 | 6 | 1 | 4 | 4 | 2 | 0 | 0 | 0 | 26 | 31 |
| Totals | 11 | 9 | 19 | 14 | 20 | 24 | 10 | 24 | 10 | 7 | 0 | 0 | 1 | 110 | 129 |

(Table 2 continued)

| Departments[a] | 1815 | | | 1816 | | | | | | | | | | | Total fourteen months |
| | Nov. | Dec. | Total | Jan. | Feb. | Mar. | Apr. | May | June | July | Aug. | Sept. | Oct. to Dec. | Total | |
|---|---|---|---|---|---|---|---|---|---|---|---|---|---|---|---|
| **Center** | | | | | | | | | | | | | | | |
| Allier | 0 | 7 | 7 | 4 | 9 | 3 | 0 | 12 | 1 | 2 | 0 | 0 | 0 | 31 | 38 |
| Cantal | 0 | 0 | 0 | 3 | 1 | 7 | 7 | 2 | 0 | 4 | 0 | 0 | 0 | 24 | 24 |
| Cher | 0 | 0 | 0 | 0 | 0 | 0 | 0 | 22 | 0 | 0 | 0 | 0 | 2 | 24 | 24 |
| Corrèze | 0 | 0 | 0 | 0 | 0 | 0 | 0 | 0 | 9 | 0 | 0 | 3 | 0 | 12 | 12 |
| Côte d'Or | 0 | 0 | 0 | 10 | 40 | 0 | 14 | 57 | 8 | 0 | 0 | 0 | 4 | 133 | 133 |
| Creuse | 9[b] | 8 | 17 | 0 | 2 | 3 | 5 | 4 | 2 | 1 | 0 | 0 | 0 | 17 | 34 |
| Haute-Loire | 7 | 1 | 8 | 9 | 17 | 4 | 6 | 28 | 0 | 0 | 0 | 0 | 0 | 64 | 72 |
| Haute-Vienne | 0 | 0 | 0 | 0 | 0 | 1 | 2 | 0 | 6 | 0 | 0 | 0 | 0 | 9 | 9 |
| Indre | 8 | 3 | 11 | 3 | 26 | 1 | 4 | 6 | 2 | 1 | 0 | 0 | 0 | 43 | 54 |
| Indre-et-Loire | 3 | 0 | 3 | 2 | 0 | 0 | 3 | 9 | 0 | 0 | 0 | 2 | 0 | 16 | 19 |
| Loir-et-Cher | 1 | 5 | 6 | 0 | 1 | 2 | 3 | 2 | 0 | 5 | 1 | 0 | 0 | 14 | 20 |
| Lot | 0 | 0 | 0 | 0 | 3 | 2 | 1 | 3 | 0 | 1 | 2 | 0 | 0 | 12 | 12 |
| Nièvre | 14 | 5 | 19 | 7 | 13 | 2 | 13 | 5 | 5 | 1 | 0 | 1 | 0 | 47 | 66 |
| Puy-de-Dôme | 0 | 0 | 0 | 1 | 1 | 4 | 4 | 3 | 1 | 0 | 0 | 0 | 0 | 14 | 14 |
| Yonne | 7[b] | 5 | 12 | 2 | 7 | 5 | 6 | 9 | 9 | 1 | 0 | 1 | 0 | 40 | 52 |
| *Totals* | 49 | 34 | 83 | 41 | 120 | 34 | 68 | 162 | 43 | 16 | 3 | 7 | 6 | 500 | 583 |

(Table 2 continued)

| Departments[a] | 1815 | | | 1816 | | | | | | | | | | | Total fourteen months |
| | Nov. | Dec. | Total | Jan. | Feb. | Mar. | Apr. | May | June | July | Aug. | Sept. | Oct. to Dec. | Total | |
|---|---|---|---|---|---|---|---|---|---|---|---|---|---|---|---|
| **North** | | | | | | | | | | | | | | | |
| Nord | 3 | 1 | 4 | 2 | 5 | 5 | 5 | 0 | 0 | 0 | 0 | 0 | 0 | 17 | 21 |
| Pas-de-Calais | 0 | 4 | 4 | 3 | 4 | 2 | 2 | 4 | 5 | 2 | 9 | 0 | 0 | 31 | 35 |
| Somme | 0 | 0 | 0 | 1 | 9 | 5 | 6 | 7 | 1 | 1 | 0 | 0 | 0 | 30 | 30 |
| *Totals* | 3 | 5 | 8 | 6 | 18 | 12 | 13 | 11 | 6 | 3 | 9 | 0 | 0 | 78 | 86 |
| **South** | | | | | | | | | | | | | | | |
| Ardèche | 1 | 0 | 1 | 11 | 0 | 2 | 0 | 4 | 0 | 0 | 0 | 0 | 0 | 17 | 18 |
| Aude | 42 | 14 | 56 | 20 | 16 | 14 | 12 | 19 | 10 | 3 | 0 | 0 | 4 | 98 | 154 |
| Bouches-du-Rhône | 5 | 0 | 5 | 4 | 1 | 0 | 1 | 0 | 2 | 0 | 0 | 1 | 0 | 9 | 14 |
| Gard | 25[b] | 2 | 27 | 6 | 1 | 1 | 0 | 9 | 5 | 4 | 2 | 1 | 1 | 30 | 57 |
| Hérault | 0 | 0 | 0 | 7 | 8 | 0 | 2 | 2 | 5 | 3 | 1 | 3 | 0 | 31 | 31 |
| Lozère | 0 | 0 | 0 | 0 | 2 | 0 | 0 | 1 | 0 | 1 | 0 | 0 | 0 | 4 | 4 |
| Pyrénées-Orientales | 13[b] | 1 | 14 | 1 | 2 | 1 | 4 | 5 | 2 | 2 | 0 | 0 | 1 | 18 | 32 |
| Tarn | 1 | 0 | 1 | 5 | 7 | 1 | 7 | 81 | 5 | 3 | 3 | 0 | 0 | 112 | 113 |
| *Totals* | 87 | 17 | 104 | 54 | 37 | 19 | 26 | 121 | 29 | 16 | 6 | 5 | 6 | 319 | 423 |

(Table 2 continued)

| Departments[a] | 1815 | | | 1816 | | | | | | | | | | | Total fourteen months |
|---|---|---|---|---|---|---|---|---|---|---|---|---|---|---|---|
| | Nov. | Dec. | Total | Jan. | Feb. | Mar. | Apr. | May | June | July | Aug. | Sept. | Oct. to Dec. | Total | |
| Southeast | | | | | | | | | | | | | | | |
| Ain | 5 | 4 | 9 | 6 | 5 | 3 | 1 | 24 | 3 | 0 | 0 | 0 | 0 | 42 | 51 |
| Basses-Alpes | 0 | 0 | 0 | 0 | 0 | 0 | 0 | 3 | 0 | 0 | 0 | 0 | 0 | 3 | 3 |
| Drôme | 3[b] | 0 | 3 | 1 | 0 | 2 | 1 | 17 | 0 | 0 | 0 | 0 | 0 | 21 | 24 |
| Hautes-Alpes | 1 | 0 | 1 | 2 | 1 | 0 | 1 | 6 | 0 | 2 | 0 | 0 | 0 | 12 | 13 |
| Isère | 11 | 8 | 19 | 11 | 11 | 15 | 6 | 75 | 19 | 5 | 0 | 4 | 6 | 152 | 171 |
| Loire | 0 | 0 | 0 | 2 | 1 | 4 | 0 | 4 | 0 | 2 | 1 | 1 | 0 | 15 | 15 |
| Rhône | 15 | 12 | 27 | 9 | 13 | 12 | 9 | 12 | 9 | 6 | 11 | 2 | 1 | 84 | 111 |
| Saône-et-Loire | 25 | 15 | 40 | 11 | 5 | 5 | 1 | 7 | 0 | 3 | 1 | 0 | 0 | 33 | 73 |
| Var | 7 | 7 | 14 | 6 | 19 | 4 | 1 | 9 | 1 | 1 | 3 | 0 | 1 | 45 | 59 |
| Vaucluse | 5[b] | 15 | 20 | 7 | 0 | 1 | 2 | 2 | 4 | 0 | 1 | 2 | 5 | 24 | 44 |
| Totals | 72 | 61 | 133 | 55 | 55 | 46 | 22 | 159 | 36 | 19 | 17 | 9 | 13 | 431 | 564 |

(Table 2 continued)

| Departments[a] | 1815 | | | 1816 | | | | | | | | | | | Total fourteen months |
|---|---|---|---|---|---|---|---|---|---|---|---|---|---|---|---|
| | Nov. | Dec. | Total | Jan. | Feb. | Mar. | Apr. | May | June | July | Aug. | Sept. | Oct. to Dec. | Total | |
| East | | | | | | | | | | | | | | | |
| Ardennes | 0 | 0 | 0 | 0 | 0 | 0 | 0 | 0 | 0 | 0 | 0 | 0 | 0 | 0 | 0 |
| Bas-Rhin | 5[b] | 1 | 6 | 3 | 2 | 7 | 1 | 8 | 4 | 0 | 1 | 0 | 0 | 26 | 32 |
| Doubs | 10[b] | 2 | 12 | 1 | 1 | 4 | 0 | 8 | 4 | 0 | 0 | 2 | 0 | 20 | 32 |
| Haute-Marne | 3 | 0 | 3 | 0 | 2 | 0 | 0 | 0 | 0 | 0 | 0 | 0 | 0 | 2 | 5 |
| Haut-Rhin | 1[b] | 0 | 1 | 0 | 3 | 0 | 0 | 3 | 0 | 1 | 0 | 0 | 0 | 7 | 8 |
| Haute-Saône | 0 | 0 | 0 | 0 | 0 | 1 | 0 | 2 | 1 | 0 | 0 | 0 | 0 | 4 | 4 |
| Jura | 34[b] | 1 | 35 | 0 | 0 | 0 | 1 | 21 | 0 | 0 | 1 | 0 | 0 | 23 | 58 |
| Marne | 0 | 3 | 3 | 0 | 6 | 1 | 0 | 3 | 3 | 5 | 0 | 0 | 0 | 18 | 21 |
| Meurthe | 0 | 1 | 1 | 4 | 0 | 0 | 1 | 0 | 0 | 0 | 0 | 0 | 5 | 10 | 11 |
| Meuse | 0 | 8 | 8 | 2 | 1 | 0 | 5 | 0 | 0 | 0 | 0 | 0 | 1 | 9 | 17 |
| Moselle | 0 | 0 | 0 | 0 | 0 | 0 | 0 | 0 | 0 | 2 | 2 | 1 | 0 | 5 | 5 |
| Vosges | 0 | 2 | 2 | 6 | 1 | 1 | 0 | 0 | 1 | 0 | 0 | 0 | 0 | 9 | 11 |
| Totals | 53 | 18 | 71 | 16 | 16 | 14 | 8 | 45 | 13 | 8 | 4 | 3 | 6 | 133 | 204 |

(Table 2 continued)

138

| Departments[a] | 1815 | | | 1816 | | | | | | | | | | | Total fourteen months |
|---|---|---|---|---|---|---|---|---|---|---|---|---|---|---|---|
| | Nov. | Dec. | Total | Jan. | Feb. | Mar. | Apr. | May | June | July | Aug. | Sept. | Oct. to Dec. | Total | |
| **West** | | | | | | | | | | | | | | | |
| Charente | 3 | 0 | 3 | 11 | 0 | 4 | 1 | 7 | 0 | 1 | 11 | 0 | 0 | 24 | 27 |
| Charente-Inférieure | 0 | 0 | 0 | 0 | 9 | 0 | 2 | 16 | 1 | 0 | 0 | 0 | 0 | 28 | 28 |
| Côtes-du-Nord | 2 | 0 | 2 | 0 | 0 | 1 | 2 | 6 | 4 | 3 | 0 | 0 | 1 | 17 | 19 |
| Deux-Sèvres | 0 | 2 | 2 | 6 | 0 | 1 | 1 | 8 | 0 | 0 | 0 | 0 | 0 | 16 | 18 |
| Finistère | 4 | 1 | 5 | 10 | 5 | 3 | 5 | 7 | 2 | 2 | 1 | 0 | 1 | 36 | 41 |
| Ille-et-Vilaine | 4 | 1 | 5 | 24 | 5 | 3 | 1 | 3 | 0 | 2 | 0 | 0 | 7 | 45 | 50 |
| Loire-Inférieure | 9[b] | 4 | 13 | 5 | 5 | 1 | 2 | 7 | 4 | 1 | 3 | 1 | 2 | 31 | 44 |
| Maine-et-Loire | 1 | 0 | 1 | 0 | 0 | 0 | 0 | 1 | 1 | 0 | 0 | 0 | 0 | 2 | 3 |
| Mayenne | 2 | 0 | 2 | 1 | 5 | 0 | 1 | 6 | 1 | 0 | 4 | 0 | 1 | 19 | 21 |
| Morbihan | 0 | 0 | 0 | 0 | 1 | 3 | 1 | 7 | 2 | 3 | 0 | 1 | 3 | 21 | 21 |
| Sarthe | 6 | 7 | 13 | 18 | 8 | 5 | 2 | 5 | 6 | 4 | 0 | 1 | 0 | 49 | 62 |
| Vendée | 0 | 1 | 1 | 5 | 3 | 4 | 2 | 2 | 3 | 0 | 0 | 0 | 0 | 19 | 20 |
| Vienne | 1 | 0 | 1 | 2 | 1 | 3 | 2 | 6 | 1 | 0 | 0 | 0 | 0 | 15 | 16 |
| *Totals* | 32 | 16 | 48 | 82 | 42 | 28 | 22 | 81 | 25 | 16 | 8 | 3 | 15 | 322 | 370 |

(Table 2 continued)

| Departments[a] | 1815 | | | 1816 | | | | | | | | | | | Total fourteen months |
|---|---|---|---|---|---|---|---|---|---|---|---|---|---|---|---|
| | Nov. | Dec. | Total | Jan. | Feb. | Mar. | Apr. | May | June | July | Aug. | Sept. | Oct. to Dec. | Total | |
| Southwest | | | | | | | | | | | | | | | |
| Ariège | 7 | 0 | 7 | 2 | 3 | 0 | 0 | 2 | 1 | 0 | 0 | 0 | 0 | 8 | 15 |
| Aveyron | 4[b] | 0 | 4 | 0 | 0 | 1 | 4 | 13 | 0 | 0 | 5 | 2 | 1 | 26 | 30 |
| Basses-Pyrénées | 3 | 5 | 8 | 10 | 6 | 22 | 5 | 20 | 8 | 5 | 6 | 0 | 0 | 82 | 90 |
| Dordogne | 1 | 0 | 1 | 1 | 7 | 6 | 24 | 0 | 0 | 0 | 0 | 0 | 0 | 38 | 39 |
| Gers | 1 | 0 | 1 | 0 | 1 | 1 | 2 | 1 | 2 | 0 | 0 | 0 | 0 | 7 | 8 |
| Gironde | 6 | 0 | 6 | 0 | 10 | 5 | 6 | 17 | 3 | 1 | 0 | 2 | 0 | 44 | 50 |
| Haute-Garonne | 4[b] | 4 | 8 | 2 | 2 | 2 | 2 | 10 | 0 | 4 | 1 | 3 | 1 | 27 | 35 |
| Hautes-Pyrénées | 5 | 6 | 11 | 2 | 10 | 7 | 2 | 5 | 6 | 1 | 0 | 2 | 0 | 35 | 46 |
| Landes | 0 | 0 | 0 | 0 | 1 | 0 | 0 | 0 | 0 | 0 | 0 | 0 | 0 | 1 | 1 |
| Lot-et-Garonne | 0 | 0 | 0 | 1 | 12 | 2 | 0 | 4 | 1 | 1 | 0 | 0 | 0 | 21 | 21 |
| Tarn-et-Garonne | 0 | 2 | 2 | 0 | 2 | 8 | 5 | 6 | 4 | 0 | 1 | 1 | 0 | 27 | 29 |
| Totals | 31 | 17 | 48 | 18 | 54 | 54 | 50 | 78 | 25 | 12 | 13 | 10 | 2 | 316 | 364 |
| Final Totals | 419 | 229 | 648 | 377 | 428 | 262 | 250 | 791 | 221 | 118 | 137 | 50 | 100 | 2734 | 3382 |

[a] Corsica omitted
[b] Includes arrests made June through October

139

# BIBLIOGRAPHY

# BIBLIOGRAPHY

The published works and archival materials listed in this bibliography are those cited in the text, with the addition of a few basic reference works. The most complete published bibliography of significance for the early Restoration is to be found in Guillaume de Bertier de Sauvigny, *Un type d'ultra-royaliste: le Comte F. de Bertier (1782–1864) et l'énigme de la Congrégation* (Paris, 1948), pp. xi–xli.

Primary and secondary sources are listed separately. The former are further subdivided into published and unpublished material. Occasional descriptive and evaluative comments indicate the significance or utility of the items listed.

## A. *Primary Sources (unpublished)*

*Note:* In the National Archives, the F series deals with police and administration, understood in a very broad sense, and the BB series concerns the courts. In the Departmental Archives, the M series deals with police and administration, and the U series with the courts.

Archives Nationales

| | | | |
|---|---|---|---|
| $BB^3123$ | $BB^{30}254$ | $F^76829$ | $F^79881$ |
| $BB^3124$ | $F^{1a}95^4$ | $F^79049$ | $F^79993$ |
| $BB^3125$ | $F^{1b}II$ | $F^79248$ | $F^79994$ |
| $BB^3126$ | $F^{1c}III$ | $F^79657$ | $F^79995$ |
| $BB^3175$ | $F^{1c}153-169$ | $F^79877$ | $F^79996$ |
| $BB^6373$ | $F^73786$ | $F^79880$ | $F^79997$ |
| $BB^{30}190$ | | | |

Archives Privées (a special section of the Archives Nationales)
Papiers Eymard
Papiers Vaublanc
These collections are recent acquisitions. I was the first researcher at the Archives Privées to examine the Papiers Vaublanc.

Archives de la Préfecture de Police, Paris.
$A^A327$
$A^A419$

# BIBLIOGRAPHY

Archives du Ministère de la Guerre (Vincennes)
$C^{18}73$
$C^{18}58$

Bibliothéque du Protestantisme Français, 3209

Bibliothèque Thiers, Fonds Masson, Carton 6

Archives Départementales du Gard
6M22

Archives du Consistoire de Nîmes

| $B53^{23}$ | $B53^{6}$ | $B53^{24}$ | $B53^{27}$ |
| $B53^{5}$ | $B53^{14}$ | | |

Archives Départementales de l'Hérault
4M52

Archives Départementales de la Haute-Garonne

| 4M33 | 4M35 | 4M147 | vU621 |
| 4M34 | 4M36 | vU620 | |

Archives Municipales de Toulouse
$I^{2}6$

The Ross reports in the British Foreign Office were communicated to me by Mrs. Alice Wemyss-Cunnack.

## B. *Primary Sources (published)*

Arbaud-Joucques, Joseph-Charles-André, Marquis d', *Troubles et agitations du département du Gard en 1815, contenant le rapport du révérend Perrot, au Comité des Ministres non-conformistes d'Angleterre, sur la prétendue persécution des Protestants en France, et sa réfutation.* Paris and Nismes, 1818.

*Archives Parlementaires de 1787 à 1860* (2ème série). Vols. XV and XVI. Paris, 1869. Reports in entirety the debates in the Chamber of Deputies and the Chamber of Peers and the texts of the bills discussed there. Volume XVI provides an index to speakers and a chronological table.

Bernis, le Comte René de, *Précis de ce qui s'est passé en 1815, dans les départemens du Gard et de la Lozère, et réfutation de plusieurs pamphlets qui ont défiguré ces événemens.* Paris and Nismes, 1818.

Beyle, Henri, *Vie de Henry Brulard* (édition Henri Martineau). Two vols. in one. Paris, 1949.

Bourchenin, Daniel, "La Terreur Blanche à Montauban et Nîmes (1815), d'après quelques lettres inédites," *Bulletin de la Société de l'histoire du Protestantisme français* (Paris), LIX (1910), 511–517.

*Bulletin des lois,* Paris, 1794– . All other collections will send one to this source eventually. The only really complete listing of laws and decrees for the Empire. It comes with useful tables bound separately. The penal code and the *Code d'Instruction criminelle* are listed under "Codes" in the Table for 1789–1814.

Combette-Caumont [*sic*], "Assassinat du Général Ramel, 15 août, 1815," *Mémoires de Tours*. Vol. III. Paris, 1837, pp. 227–280.

Connac, E., "La réaction royaliste à Toulouse: Trois lettres inédites de Picot de Lapeyrouse . . ." *Revue des Pyrénées*, X (1898), 431–451.

Constant, Benjamin, *Lettres à M. Charles Durand, avocat, en réponse aux questions contenues dans . . . Marseille, Nismes et ses environs en 1815.* Paris, 1818.

*Défense des Protestants du Bas-Languedoc.* 1815. Probably published in Nîmes. Defends the Protestants as loyal to the Bourbons.

Durand, Charles, *Marseille, Nîmes et ses environs en 1815.* Paris, 1818.

Lauze de Peret, P. J., *Causes et précis des crimes, des désordres dans le département du Gard et dans d'autres lieux du Midi de la France en 1815 et en 1816.* Paris, 1819.

*Le Moniteur.* The official newspaper. Important for appointments, the publication of decrees, and so on.

Perrot, Clement, Rev., *Report on the Persecutions of the French Protestants. Presented to the Committee of Dissenting Ministers of the Three Denominations in and about the Cities of London and Westminister.* London, 1816.

Pasquier, Etienne-Denis de, *Histoire de mon temps. Mémoires du Chancelier Pasquier.* Vols. III and IV. Paris, 1894.

Rémusat, Charles de, *Mémoires de ma vie.* Vol. I: *Enfance et jeunesse; la Restauration.* Edited by Charles Pouthas. Paris, 1958. With the explanation supplied, in footnotes, by Charles Pouthas, of persons, places, and events mentioned in the text, this has been made a superb source for the political, cultural and social life of the Restoration.

Villèle, Joseph de, *Mémoires et Correspondance du Comte de Villèle.* Vol. I. Paris, 1888. This is the first volume of five that cover the period of the Restoration.

Vitrolles, Eugène François de, *Mémoires et relations politiques.* Vols. II and III. Paris, 1884. An impassioned account of treason and heroism, the latter the author's own.

Wellesley, Arthur, Duke of Wellington, *Supplementary Despatches, Correspondence, and Memoranda.* Vol. XI. London, 1863. This is an important source for political developments in France.

## C. *Reference Works*

*Almanach impérial.* Paris, 1814; *Almanach royal.* Paris, 1815. Extremely useful for administrative organization and personnel, rough population data, even travel time between major cities in France. Its title changes with regimes.

# BIBLIOGRAPHY

Bastid, Paul, *Les institutions politiques de la monarchie parlementaire française (1814-1848)*. Paris, 1954.

Bérenger, Alphonse, *De la justice criminelle en France, d'après les lois permanentes, les lois d'exception, et les doctrines des tribunaux*. Paris, 1818.

*Dictionnaire des communes, administratif et militaire*. 21st ed. revised. Edited by Le Commandant Repain. Paris, 1938. This has served as a guide to the proper spelling and proximity to urban centers of certain rural communes.

*Documents statistiques sur la France*. Publiés par le ministère du Commerce. Paris, 1835.

Esmein, Adhémar, *Histoire de la procédure criminelle en France et spécialement de la procédure inquisitive, depuis le XIII siècle jusqu'à nos jours*. Paris, 1882.

Godechot, Jacques, *Les institutions de la France sous la Révolution et l'Empire*. Paris, 1951.

Michaud (ed.), *Biographie universelle, ancienne et moderne*. New revised edition, 45 vols. Paris 186? –     .

Robert, Adolphe, Edgar Bourloton, and Gaston Cougny, *Dictionaire des parlementaires français*. 5 vols. Paris, 1889–1891.

## D.  *Secondary Sources*

Aldéguier, A. d', *Histoire de la ville de Toulouse*. 4 vols. Toulouse, 1833–1835.

Alleaume, Charles, "La Terreur Blanche dans le Var," *Bulletin de la Société d'études scientifiques et archéologiques de Draguignan*, XLV (1944–45), 5–27.

André, Robert, *L'occupation de la France par les alliés en 1815 (juillet-novembre)*. Paris, 1924.

Baragnon, P. L., *Abrégé de l'histoire de Nismes, de Menard; continué jusqu'à nos jours*. Vol. IV. Nismes, 1835.

Bécarud, Jean, "La noblesse dans les Chambres (1815–1830)," *Revue internationale d'histoire politique et constitutionelle* (Paris), Nouvelle série, no. 11 (juillet-septembre, 1953), pp. 189–205.

Bertier de Sauvigny, Guillaume de, *Un type d'ultra-royaliste: le Comte Ferdinand de Bertier (1782–1864) et l'énigme de la Congrégation*. Paris, 1948.

—— *La Restauration*. Paris, 1955; 2 ed. rev., Paris, 1964.

—— "F. de Bertier, Préfet du Calvados," *Bulletin de la Société des Antiquaires de Normandie*, 1959, pp. 13–261.

Busquet, Raoul, *Histoire de Marseille*. Paris, 1945.

Causse, Henri, "Un industriel Toulousain au temps de la Révolution et de l'Empire: François-Bernard Boyer-Fonfrède (1767–?)," *Annales du Midi*, LXIX (1957), 121–133.

Claudon, Ferdinand, "La cour prévôtale de la Côte d'Or (1816–1818),"

# BIBLIOGRAPHY

*Bulletin du Comité des travaux historiques* (Paris), X (1924), section histoire moderne et contemporaine, pp. 95–132.

Crouzet, François, "Le sous-développement économique du sud-ouest," *Annales du Midi,* LXXI (1959), 71–79.

Daudet, Ernest, *La Terreur Blanche: Episodes et souvenirs de la réaction dans le midi en 1815.* 2nd ed. Paris, 1906.

Dumolard, Henry, *Jean-Paul Didier et la conspiration de Grenoble, 4 mai, 1816: la terreur blanche dans l'Isère.* Grenoble, 1928.

Duvergier de la Hauranne, Prosper, *Histoire du gouvernement parlementaire en France.* Vol. III. Paris, 1859.

———ed., *Mémoires posthumes de Odillon Barrot.* Vol. I. Paris, 1875.

Fourcassié, Jean, *Villèle.* Paris, 1954.

Gaffarel, Paul, "Un épisode de la Terreur Blanche: Les massacres de Marseille en juin, 1815," *La Révolution Française,* XLIX (1905), 317–350.

——— "L'occupation étrangère à Marseille en 1815," *La Révolution Française,* LII (1907), 523–543; LIII (1907), 43–71.

Godechot, Jacques, *La Contre-révolution, 1789–1804.* Paris, 1961.

Greer, Donald, *The Incidence of the Terror during the French Revolution: A Statistical Interpretation.* Cambridge, Mass., 1935.

Gwynn, Lewis, "La Terreur blanche et l'application de la loi Decazes dans le département du Gard (1815–1817)," *Annales Historiques de la Révolution Française* (April–June, 1964), 174–193.

Hémardinquer, J. J., "Affaires et politique sous la monarchie censitaire; Un libéral: F.-B. Boyer-Fonfrède (1767–1845), *Annales du Midi,* LXXIII (1961), 165–218.

Houssaye, Henry, *1815.* Vol. I: *La première restauration: Le retour de l'île d'Elbe.* 10th ed., rev. Paris, 1893. Vol. III: *La seconde abdication: La terreur blanche.* 50th ed., rev. Paris, 1911.

Kurtz, Harold, *The Trial of Marshal Ney: His Last Years and Death.* New York, 1957.

Lautard, Laurent, *Esquisses historiques: Marseille depuis 1789 jusqu'en 1815.* Vol. II. Marseille, 1844.

Leuilliot, Paul, *L'Alsace au début du XIXe siècle.* Vol. I: *La vie politique.* Paris, 1959.

Ligou, Daniel, "La structure sociale du Protestantisme Montalbanais à la fin du XVIIIe siècle," *Bibliothèque de la Société de l'histoire du Protestantisme français,* C (1954), 93–110.

Loubet, Jean, "Le gouvernement Toulousain du Duc d'Angoulême après les Cent Jours," *La Révolution Française,* XIV (1913), 149–165, 337–366.

Madelin, Louis, *Fouché, 1759–1820.* 2nd ed., rev. 2 vols. Paris, 1903.

Marjolin, Robert, "Troubles provoqués en France par la disette de 1816–17," *Revue d'histoire moderne,* VIII (1933), 423–460.

Mellon, Stanley, *The Political Uses of History: A Study of Historians in the French Restoration.* Stanford, 1958.

Paillet, André, "Les cours prévôtales (1816–18)," *Revue des Deux Mondes,* IV (1911), 123–149.

Poland, Burdette, *French Protestants and the French Revolution.* Princeton, 1957.

Ponteil, Félix, *La chute de Napoléon et la crise française de 1814–15.* Paris, 1943.

Pouthas, Charles, *Guizot pendant la Restauration: Préparation de l'homme d'état* (1814–1830). Paris, 1923.

——— *La population française pendant la première moitié du XIXe siècle.* Paris, 1956.

——— *Histoire politique de la restauration.* Mimeographed. Paris, n.d.

Praviel, Armand, "Le massacre de Ramel," *Oeuvres Libres* (Paris), LXXVIII (1927), 269–320.

Ramet, Henri, "Les cours prévôtales dans le ressort de la Cour d'appel de Toulouse," *Recueil de l'Académie de Législation de Toulouse,* 4e série, VIII (1929), 1–41.

Rémond, René, *La droite en France, de 1815 à nos jours.* Paris, 1954.

Robert, Daniel, *Les Eglises Réformées en France (1800–1830).* Paris, 1961.

Sancti, L., "Notes et documents sur les intrigues royalistes dans le Midi de la France de 1792 à 1815," *Mémoires de l'Académie des Sciences de Toulouse,* IV (1916), 37–114.

Siegfried, André, "Le groupe Protestant Cévenol sous la IIIe République," in Marc Boegner et al., *Protestantisme français.* ("Présences" series.) Paris, 1945.

Spitzer, Alan, "The Bureaucrat as Proconsul: The Restoration Prefect and the *Police Générale,*" *Comparative Studies in Society and History,* VII (1965), 371–392.

Thiry, Jean, *La seconde abdication de Napoléon Ier.* Paris, 1945.

——— *Les débuts de la Deuxième Restauration.* Paris, 1947.

"Un chapitre inconnu de l'affaire Ramel," *Revue historique de Toulouse,* XXIII (1936), 225–237.

Vaulabelle, Achille de, *Histoire des Deux Restaurations jusqu'à la chute de Charles X.* 2nd ed. Vols. IV and V. Paris, 1847.

Vidalenc, Jean, "La cour prévôtale des Bouches-du-Rhône (1815–1817)," *Congrès des Sociétés Savantes de Paris et des départements.* Toulouse, 1953.

——— "La vie économique des départements mediterranéens pendant l'Empire," *Revue d'histoire moderne et contemporaine,* I (1954), 165–198.

——— *Les demi-solde: Etude d'une catégorie sociale.* Paris, 1955. Tables indicate the number and dispersion of these former officers.

Wemyss, Alice, "L'Angleterre et la Terreur blanche de 1815 dans le Midi," *Annales du Midi,* LXXIII (1961), 287–311.

Wolff, Philippe, *Histoire de Toulouse.* Toulouse, 1958.

# INDEX

149

# INDEX

Cambrai, 66-67, 68
Canuel, General, 76
Cardonnel (legislative committee member), 72, 80
Carnot, Lazare, 69
Cateau-Cambrésis, 66
Cavalier, M., 53, 54
Central Government of the Midi (Gouvernement Central du Midi), 3, 23
Cévennes, 42, 46, 56, 59
*Chambre introuvable,* 32, 33-34, 40, 63; dissolution of, 115
Charles X, 119
Charter of *1814,* 1, 23, 39, 61, 74, 77, 83, 85, 119, 120
Chartran, Sébastien, General, 76
Chateau d'If, 14, 100
Chazelles, Count de, 23-24
Chevaliers de la Foi, 34, 38, 116, 117; history of, 24-25; and liberation of Toulouse (*1814*), 26; and Ramel murder, 36; and Chamber of Deputies, 40, 64, 65; in Arles, Nîmes and Marseilles, 47
Chifflet (deputy), 72
Civil liberties, 77-78. *See also* Trial, jury
Combettes-Caumont (counselor, *cour royale*), 34-37
Commère (Ramel murder trial witness), 35-37, 38
Confédération du Midi, 29
Constant, Benjamin, 61-62
Continental Blockade, 5, 21
Contraband, 97
Corbière, Jacques-Joseph de, 72, 73, 75
Cotton (deputy), 72
Cuvier, Georges, 89
Courts, *see* Ordinary Court; Provost Court; Special courts

Dalmatia, Soult, Marshal, Duke of, 85
Damas-Crux, Duke of, 6, 28n, 36, 38
Dambray, Charles-Henri, 66, 85
Daudet, Ernest, 116, 117
Daunant (mayor of Nîmes), 45, 46
Decaen, General, 23, 24, 27
Decazes, Elie, 77, 103-104
Delpuch, M., 54

Demi-solde, 52; and law on administrative arrests, 109
Detention, power of, 77; and law on administrative arrests, 100-103
Didier, Jean-Paul, 106, 115
Donnadieu, General, 106
Duplessis de Grenedan (deputy), 88-90
Duvergier de Hauranne (deputy), 72, 74

Elections, 32-34, 38, 40, 63
Emigrés, in Chamber of Deputies, 63
Exmouth, Lord, 8

*Fédérations,* 17, 29, 47, 52
*Fédérés,* 18, 28, 30, 54
Feltre, Clarke, Henri-Jacques, Duke of, 75, 76, 86, 87, 91
Figueras, Spain, 3, 28
Fortress prisons, 14, 100
Fouché, Joseph, 38, 67-68, 70, 77, 101-102, 103

Gard, 6, 7, 15, 40; religious persecution in, 41-62, 116; disarmament in, 56-57
*Gardes royaux secrets, see* Secrets
Garnier de Saintes (Convention member), 69
Germiny (deputy), 72
Gilly, General, 3, 46-49, 70
Government personnel, *see* Officeholders
Grain, 21, 55, 94
Great Britain, 22; Fleet of, 4, 8; and amnesty proposals, 67, 70
Guizot, François, 80

Henri IV, 75
Hood, Admiral, 8
Hudson-Lowe, General, 16
Humbert de Sesmaisons (deputy), 82
Hyde de Neuville, Jean-Guillaume, 79, 90

Import-export patterns, 5, 21
Imprisonments: in Marseilles, 12-13; in Toulon, 17; in Avignon, 18; in Toulouse, 29-30. *See also* Arrests

# INDEX

Informers, 28, 29
Institut Philanthropique, 25

Jolivet (deputy), 80
Judicial reform, 100. *See also* Provost
    Courts

Kléber, Jean-Baptiste, General, 10

La Bourdonnaye, François-Régis de, 64;
    and amnesty decree, 71-76 *passim*
Lagarde, General, 58
Languedoc, 3, 15, 37, 39-40, 116; eco-
    nomic decline in, 5; topography, 6
La Palud, Truce of, 3, 23
La Rivière, Charles-François, Marquis
    de, 8, 13, 15, 18
Legislation, 1; initiative in, 65-66. *See
    also* Administrative arrests, law on
*L'Independant* (newspaper), 68
Lepelletier (Convention member), 69
*Lettre de cachet,* 100
Limayrac, Charles-Antoine de, 26, 40
Lord's Prayer, 98
Louis XVI, 68, 69
Louis XVIII, 23, 44; in Ghent, 1-2, 6;
    returns to Paris, 7, 16, 24; and special
    delegates, 36-37, 39; and legislature
    "introuvable," 63; and amnesty pro-
    posals, 66-67; and amnesty decree,
    68-70; dissolves Chamber, 115
Lowe, Sir Hudson, *see* Hudson-Lowe,
    General

MacCarthy, Robert, 36, 40
Magistrates, *see* Officeholders
Malaret, Baron Joseph de, 25, 32, 36
Manuel, Jacques-Antoine, 68n
Marie-Louise, 106
Marie-Thérèse Regiment, 28, 35
Mamelukes, 10-11
Mayors, *see* Officeholders
Messey, Maréchal de Camp de, 94-95
Ministers, responsibilities of, 65-66, 119
Montcalm, Marquis de, 15
Mouton-Duvernet, General, 76-77
Murard de Saint, Romain (deputy), 89-
    90

Napoleon II, 16, 48, 106

National guards, 31, 105; of Marseilles,
    9; of Avignon, 18; of Toulouse, 27-
    28, 35; of Nîmes, 42, 46, 49, 50, 52,
    57, 58, 59; of Beaucaire, 49
Ners, 56
Ney, Michel, Marshal, 70, 71

Occupation, military, 17n; Austrian, 16-
    17, 56; Prussian, 38
Officeholders, purge of, 11-12, 48, 108-
    109, 118; magistrates, 13-14, 16, 53-
    54, 91; mayors, 25-26, 49; subpre-
    fects, 48; customs officials, 97; tax
    collectors, 97
Ordinary courts, political convictions
    in, 111-114

Pardessus (deputy), 72, 80
Pasquier, Etienne-Denis, Baron, 12, 81,
    96, 102
Penal code, 78, 79; defines subversion,
    110-111
Peninsular War (*1808-1814*), 21
Pérignon, Dominique de, Marshal, 15,
    27; and Ramel's assassination, 33
Perrot, Clément, 50, 53n, 55n, 60n
Piet (Parisian deputy), 65, 82
Priests, 109-110
Prisons, *see* Fortress prisons; Imprison-
    ments
Protestants, English, 59-61
Protestants, French, 89, 116; population
    distribution and wealth, 41-42; under
    old regime, 42, 44; and revolution-
    ary and Napoleonic legislation, 42-
    43; acquisition of Church property
    by, 43; religious processions enjoined
    by, 43-44; political power of, 43-45,
    53; exodus from Nîmes, 54-55
Provence, 3, 5-19, 37, 116; economic
    decline of, 5; topography of, 6; and
    purge of government personnel, 12
Provost courts, 83-99; reestablishment
    of, 82, 84-85, 86; history of, 83-84,
    87; and sedition act, 86, 87, 96; bill
    introduced, 86-87; passage of law,
    87-90; staffing problems, 88-89, 90-
    92; begin to function, 90; limits of,
    93-95; activity of, 96-98; penalties

# HARVARD HISTORICAL STUDIES